1/5/2016

Dear Nick,

This book will set the stage for your next step. "Where there is a will, there is a way". Good Luck as you finish up Del. Please + Thank you

MWB

The Flow of Life

KEEPING YOUR DREAM ALIVE

Eric I. Mitchell MD

authorHOUSE

AuthorHouse™
1663 Liberty Drive
Bloomington, IN 47403
www.authorhouse.com
Phone: 1 (800) 839-8640

© 2015 Eric I. Mitchell MD. All rights reserved.

No part of this book may be reproduced, stored in a retrieval system, or transmitted by any means without the written permission of the author.

Published by AuthorHouse 09/24/2015

ISBN: 978-1-5049-5154-8 (sc)
ISBN: 978-1-5049-5152-4 (hc)
ISBN: 978-1-5049-5153-1 (e)

Library of Congress Control Number: 2015915648

Print information available on the last page.

Any people depicted in stock imagery provided by Thinkstock are models, and such images are being used for illustrative purposes only.
Certain stock imagery © Thinkstock.

This book is printed on acid-free paper.

Because of the dynamic nature of the Internet, any web addresses or links contained in this book may have changed since publication and may no longer be valid. The views expressed in this work are solely those of the author and do not necessarily reflect the views of the publisher, and the publisher hereby disclaims any responsibility for them.

Contents

Dedication vii
Acknowledgements ix
Foreword xi

Chapter One 1
Early Days

Chapter Two 9
DeMatha High School

Chapter Three 17
College Bound—St. Joseph's University

Chapter Four 27
Leadership—Part 1

Chapter Five 33
Medical School—University of Pennsylvania

Chapter Six 38
Staying in the Game

Chapter Seven 43
Future Look

Chapter Eight 47
Becoming a Leader

Chapter Nine 54
Internship and Ben Casey

Chapter Ten 60
Orthopaedic Sojourn

Chapter Eleven 65
Short Detour

Chapter Twelve..70
Sports Medicine/E-M Angle

Chapter Thirteen..77
Time for Pro Forma

Chapter Fourteen..82
Practice/Service to My Country

Chapter Fifteen..87
Life Outside Medicine

Chapter Sixteen..94
My Country Calls

Chapter Seventeen..98
Call-to-Duty

Chapter Eighteen..105
Leadership Part 2

Chapter Nineteen..108
Military Promotion

Chapter Twenty..115
The Press

Chapter Twenty-One..125
New Command to War

Chapter Twenty-Two..135
Return from War

Chapter Twenty-Three...139
Team Vision to ACtioN

Dedication

With love and deep affection I dedicate this book to my sister, Diane Juanita Cecelia Mitchell.

As a young second grader at the age of seven, Diane inspired me to believe in myself and to never allow anyone or anything—even inevitable setbacks—to distract me from achieving my goals. Throughout my life and until her death on January 17, 2014, she believed in my ability to conquer any challenge that I faced. I knew she had my back. She will live on in my mind and heart forever.

Eric Ignatius Mitchell, MD MA FACPE CPE

Livermore Falls, Maine

June 9, 2015

Acknowledgements

There are many beginnings throughout life. It is what you do with them that matters.

First and foremost, all my love goes to my wife, Carmen, who has been there for me through "thick and thin" for many years now. Her love and support has meant the world to me. Without her, this book would not be published.

It is one thing to have an idea for a book, another to get it down on paper. For this, a special thank you goes to Doreen Alexander, who was there from the start with her ideas, expertise and editing skills.

Speaking of beginnings, Melinda Miller, my right-arm person, has been with me since I started in medical practice some thirty years ago. Her devotion to developing my career and staunch support of me over the years is beyond measure. Melinda has had an integral part in the editing and formatting of the final draft manuscript.

My sons, Justin Ignatius and Marcus Alexander, are my pride and joy. Justin, the writer in the family, read the manuscript and made suggestions. My now daughters, Isabella and Brianna, are the light of my life.

My love goes to my sisters and brother for the wonderful memories of times well spent.

It goes without saying that many, many additional people over the years have contributed greatly to the creation of the wonderful life I have and the man I have become today. To mention them all would be impossible. You know who you are…..Siempre

Foreword
By Morgan Wootten

Coaching was, has been and still is my life. I do not coach basketball any more after forty-six years of coaching for a single high school but I still coach. Coaching is a lifelong practice of teaching a single person or a group of people in a given sports or discipline.

There are so many life lessons when you can pour a little of what you know into another person so willing to know what you know. Near the end of my coaching career, I had the pleasure of writing a book, titled A Coach for All Seasons. In that book, I selected three players who resonated with me during my successful coaching sojourn. Those three players were not chosen because of their basketball ability but were selected because what they brought to the game as part and parcel of whom they were, and why they were winners then and now.

It is almost twenty years since I had the pleasure of writing that book. Now, I have the pleasure of writing a foreword for one of those three players who continues to exhibit the values that he brought to the hardwood, now over fifty years ago.

Vision and personal values are characteristics that are timeless. When you take that vision to action with the personal values that were anchored in a strong faith and family background, then you have a foundation to build a productive, successful and happy life.

When this young man, a late bloomer from a basketball perspective, stepped onto the basketball court for that first day of practice, I knew he was a diamond in the rough, waiting to be buffed to a high shine. That is a coach's dream!

It is my pleasure to have a belated hand in introducing to you the story of Dr. Eric I. Mitchell—a story worth telling of a young man's struggle to beat the odds and accomplish all of his goals and dreams. This is a story worth telling because it lends the ways, means and ends of how you can keep your dream, whatever it is, alive. Why was his WHY so Important? Dr. Mitchell, aka Eric, repeatedly in each chapter of this book and in each chapter of his life showed why the formation of your WHY is so critical to one's success.

Every teen, student, student athlete from Generation X and present millennials should make this book a-must-read. You will be inspired by his story to a point of focusing on your life.

Chapter One

This book is written with the poem, IF, by Rudyard Kipling (1865-1936), profoundly recorded in the back of my mind—a life lesson tool given me by my father. The many other wise sayings of my father allow their eternal impact to shine through the pages of this book.

The early days with my family in Clinton, Maryland, were good, bad, and ugly. The good days would be talking about the garden that we had in the back of the house. It would be about the fact that five of us at that time slept in one room; bunk beds were the order of the day. I had the upper bunk and rolled off it almost every night and hit the floor. My dad would come in and pick me up and put me back. Many times I would not even wake up.

Some of the bad happened when my mother and father would have words. It would be loud. The ugly occurred when my mom left my dad, and I had to go with her and not be with my dad. I didn't want to go; however, my dad came and got me every weekend, no matter what. I was in third grade when this happened. From the time that I started school, I had a tough time reading and spelling. I also stuttered very badly.

The story of where we went after we left Clinton, Maryland, will be told as we moved into the projects in SE Washington, DC. The good part there was that I was near my first cousin and he was my age. This was good because we played together; my little brother was just two years old and too young to play with.

We were not there very long before we moved to northeast Washington, DC. We moved into a house that had more than two bedrooms. Here, I had my own room. I went to a public school for the fourth grade. It was the first time I went to a school with white kids. During all my years in Maryland, we were forced to go to separate schools.

Church was different because my father was a pit bull about his religion. He would not back down under any condition. He believed that God created us all in his likeness and image. The priest of the church told my father that my sister and I would have to walk in the back of the line for our first Holy Communion. Well, Dad wrote a letter to the Archbishop of Washington which became my "Mission to Equality" because my sister and I ended up walking in our respective places in line. We bypassed the "Colored Pew" in the back of the Church and sat in the first row every Sunday. Dad always said, "Sometimes you have to overdo a point to make a point."

Washington, DC—a new house; a new school; and, an apple tree to climb in the backyard made life interesting. Being with dad on the weekends was fun because I got to walk in the woods near our old house and hunt with my 22 rifle. There was a school change after the first year in Washington where we went from public school to Catholic school. Dad thought it was the most important thing in living the American dream.

Moving from my first integrated school system of a 50/50 racial split, I would now go to my first year in Catholic school and become a minority again on the other end of the spectrum. In two years, I had come from an all-black school system as one of many to an almost all-white school, being one of a few black students.

The Flow of Life

Things did not go so well the first year in Catholic school. With my slow start from my first grade, three-room schoolhouse, I got D's and F's my first year in Catholic school and thought that it meant 'Doing Fine'. Wrong! Well, with a repeat of the fifth grade, I had to get serious and I did. I turned those D's and F's into A's and B's.

I would start my sports history with the Catholic Youth Organization (CYO) football as a tight end. This went on from the sixth to the eighth grade. I was tall and skinny and didn't set the world on fire. Girls became an interest and Yolanda took me almost one mile out of my way home as I would walk her home after school.

My testing skills were still not good when I took my entrance examination for Catholic high school. The result proved it. I didn't get into any of my selected schools. I was in limbo. Every Catholic high school was designed as all girls or all boys at that time. At fourteen years of age and with a new-found interest in girls, this was not considered such a bad thing.

The events of that summer would prove to be earth-moving in my life. My mother married again and we moved into a new house. My mother's mother, my four sisters, and my little brother were all a part of this new matrix. The chemistry in this new abode was not good. I was neither tied to a school nor the new house that was called home. I still saw my dad every weekend.

I turned fifteen years old on the first day of August that summer. I knew that I needed my dad and not this new "imposter" who didn't measure up in any way, shape, or form. I packed a few things and left for my journey of about ten miles across the landscape of Washington, DC, back to Capitol Heights, Maryland, to my father's apartment.

Dad was a United States Postal Service mail clerk who sorted mail on a train from Washington, DC, to New York City. This was an eight days on five days off job. He would work eight days working on the train, sorting mail grabbed along this route from Washington, to NYC, stay overnight in NYC and return to DC for one day. Then, he would do it again before he would have a schedule that gave him five to seven days off. Then he was back on the train to NYC. No fair warning was possible of my cross-town sojourn for my dad because he was in New York City the day I abdicated from the mother country. There were no cell phones, texting or e-mails in those days.

I knew his schedule like it was mine. I knew that he would return in the early am of the next morning of August 2nd. I had my apartment key and with a skilled hand of hitch hiking, I made it to dad's place. All was well until a knock came at the door about eight hours after my arrival. I didn't open the door but asked who was there. "It's the State Police," was the response. I still didn't open the door but asked if I could help them. They asked if I was Eric and I affirmed that I was. They stated that my mother reported me a run-a-way. I explained that I couldn't be much of a run-a-way when I was at my dad's place. I never opened the door. They asked me to call my mother. I guess my bass voice at fifteen years of age told a lot of the story.

Well, about 2:30 am brought the arrival of dad, home from his two-day jaunt from New York City and the United States Postal Service. I was a big surprise for him. He woke me and put forth the proverbial question, "What are you doing here?" I was glad to see him and got up and had tea with him. It was his drink of habit. I explained that with the new husband and six women, home was not the place I needed to be. I told him that I needed to be with him. He

The Flow of Life

was quick to explain that he didn't have anyone to take care of me when he was on his New York run.

I think I have denoted that this was my fifteenth birthday week. I was now about six feet, three inches tall. My bass in my voice was the reverse of my height. My answer to my daddy's dilemma was my request for a caregiver, brunette in nature, about five feet eight inches tall, 36-24-36. Dad was quick to move away from this subject to remind me of how much of a disciplinarian he was and I would have to walk a very straight line. He announced that dust was not allowed to hit the floor. I took his challenge and told him that I would catch the dust before it hit the floor.

After dad talked to mom the next morning, dad did what he knew was best. We set up housekeeping and all the ground rules were established. Now, I had one month to get ready for school. I signed up for the local high school which was only at the top of the hill, less than a half-mile away. I had friends already because I spent every weekend with dad. That was easy. Now, in short order, I would be going to school with these buddies and girls.

I had to go and see my mother at least once every ten to twelve days. I didn't stay over but just went to visit. School started and I was quick to discover that this high school would not get me into college. I had cycled 360 degrees in the Brown vs the Board of Education. I had started my education in a three-room schoolhouse separate but equal make-up which was the law of the land. In 1954, the Supreme Court overturned Plessy vs Ferguson (1896), in a decision where the Supreme Court denoted separation by race was still equal in education. Well, this was not true. This overturn of this fifty-two year old law had me now enrolled in a multicultural, multiracial school from the fourth grade going forward in my flow of life in America.

On my return to Maryland, now living with my dad, I was at a school where political gerrymandering had me once again back at a 99.1% black school. I had lived this history and studied this history in school, but it was upon my return to this high school that I clearly understood that separate was not equal. In the ninth grade, I was being introduced to course material that I had studied twice in the fifth grade, and some of the content was from my sixth grade classes. Within two weeks, I told my dad that I had to go back to Catholic school and leave the girls if I ever wanted to go to college and on to medical school. I explained the difference that I saw in the two education systems. I had lived it. My father was quick to answer and said that I should take the entry examination again. He also said, "When you get in, I will find a way to pay for it." This school year had a lot of A's and B's with a dose of student council and drama and a flash of basketball. I was now about six feet four-inches tall with a deep desire to play basketball. I only got to run the court twice before the basketball coach requested that I grab the rim from a standing position. I couldn't do it. My audition was short lived and I was relegated back to the local outdoors basketball courts for more lessons to be learned.

However, my desire remained intact and was intensified with that short fall of not being able to grab the basketball rim when a respected high school basketball coach thought with my height I should have had that ability at a minimum. And dad always said, "Never let someone's minimum be your maximum." I would practice jumping every day in the apartment, trying to have my head touch the ceiling of the eight foot six inch ceiling. I will tell you that in a

The Flow of Life

short period of time I reached that goal and then had to be careful not to drive my head through the ceiling or even break my neck. I changed my location for my target jumping thereafter, where I had no glass or manmade ceilings on my ability to jump out of the gym.

My dad posed the question shortly after Christmas of that year and that was would I like to see a high school basketball player who was seven feet one inch tall. This basketball phenomenon was coming to play against a local Catholic high school. My response was a quick, "Yes, please, and thank you." Game time came. We sat up high in a sold-out Maryland Cole Field House with 13,500 fans in attendance. The electricity in the air was unbelievable that night. The outcome was in favor of the big guy from New York, but the local team had hit a cord with me. As my father and I drove home in the recent snowstorm, I told my dad that I was going to go to the same Catholic high school and I was going to play basketball for them. My father was quick to stop me, and suggested that I remember why I was going to go back to Catholic school from the present public school. He denoted that first things were first. If my studies were in order, I could play any sport I desired.

My target jumping continued to improve by leaps and bounds as I prepared for my delayed entry examination for admission into Catholic high school. I marked DeMatha Catholic High School as my number one choice for entry. I took the examination, passed and got my first choice. I was on my way to DeMatha Catholic High School. My father made me take a typing course that summer at DeMatha. I thank him for that to this day.

The first day of school had started. It was a shirt, tie, and jacket dress code with my shoes to a spit shine because I lived with the former First Sgt., veteran, United States Army World War II. He denoted that you could determine a man by his shoes and mine always had to be Right- Dress- Right. Dad's mantra was "you never get a second chance to make a first impression."

Chapter Two

I was walking in the halls of DeMatha Catholic High School on the first day of school when an outstretched hand fell upon my shoulder. I turned my now six foot five inch body to a friendly face that asked me my name. I hadn't had enough time to break any of these new rules within the school. So, I answered with confidence, "I am Eric I. Mitchell." The next question was, "Do you play basketball?" My answer was "Yes." This time, I had been asked a simple question without any validating basketball task attached. The smiling face said, "I am Morgan Wootten, the basketball coach, and I would like to see you out on the floor the first day of basketball practice." I assured him that I would be there.

School started anew from Section C of the tenth grade at DeMatha Catholic High School. This was not a college-prep track section like tracks A and B, but I was allowed to request and take courses outside of my home room of Section C. So, I did just that and fashioned my courses with college in mind. By my senior year, every course I was taking was not in Section track C but tracks B or A.

The first day of B-Ball practice was about to change my life. My abilities as a basketball player were about to reflect the players who were on the court. I had a lot of desire and the assistant coach picked up on my raw talent, or the lack thereof. He asked if I was willing to work an extra twenty minutes every day to improve my skills. I accepted this offer in a heartbeat.

Frank was the name of the assistant coach. He was the biggest white man I had ever known. Frank might not have been the biggest white man in the world, but in my eyes, he was about six feet eight inches tall with the biggest hands and feet I had ever seen. Frank worked with me every day after the regular practice and modified my jumping program and showed me how to jump from down low. Grabbing the rim was now child's play. Frank made it clear that the game of basketball was to be played above the rim, and that's where I needed to live, above the rim.

After months of working with Coach Frank, I could now elevate to above the rim. I could now dunk the basketball one or two handed. He taught me how to go to a spot on the floor where the action would be in the coming seconds—anticipation. He taught me to watch every pass, every shot, and determine where the next pass or shot was coming from. With this information, I could determine where the shot was long or short and start moving for that rebound before the ball even hit the rim. I improved with every game. Our team was to get another opportunity at this seven foot one inch player and his team from NYC. Coach Wootten had a tennis racket which was held up in shooting drills because even our biggest and tallest guy didn't have the wing span of their star.

We had a better outcome this year with a victory over this NYC team, and DeMatha was raised to national prominence for high school basketball. Oh, what a difference a year can make! The college coaches flocked to our school before that game. Now, with a number one ranking, the race was on. In my junior year, I took on a sixth-man role, where I would come off the bench and inject my energy into the game: two steals, one offensive charge, two offensive rebounds, and

The Flow of Life

four to six points, to give DeMatha another win. My name started showing up in the sports section week after week.

The letters of recruitment for basketball started to come from every size and shape of colleges and universities across the country. Coach Wootten laid down all the rules that we were to follow in meetings with coaching and traveling to schools for recruiting trips. Coach Wootten already had national recognition as one of the top high school basketball coaches in the country. So here I was with two blessings, a stellar head basketball coach, and the best big man assistant coach with private lessons wrapped into one program. Me, I was doing what my dad had denoted that snowy night as we drove home from my first encounter with DeMatha basketball. I kept my studies up, and I was taking more and more college-bound courses outside of my Track C homeroom, and playing any sport I wanted to.

Vietnam was starting to heat up as I worked my way through high school. The Selective Service Board had just changed the drafting process from oldest in a family to a by date of birth process. Every young man at the age of eighteen years was to sign up with their local Selective Service Board. This new system was a lottery-type system where a number was attached to each day of the year. The unlucky day was Sept 27th which got the number one spot for recruitment into the Armed Forces.

Three hundred-sixty-five balls were put into the bowl with a day and month. If your date of birth ball was day 200 or greater, it was a very safe bet that you were not going to be drafted unless there was a World War III. My draft number was 112 which corresponded to my August 1st birthday, not so lucky.

There was another provision which could also keep you out of a very unpopular war. If you went to college full time after high school, you would receive a deferral from the draft until completion of your four years of college provided you were a full time student. Part-time students were not exempt. Most of my Track C classmates were not headed to college like I was. A number of classmates went and others signed up because of their low numbers in the draft, others were drafted, and a few would cross the border into Canada. X was the number that went to Vietnam and X was the number that came home. A few of my homeroom pals came home with more problems than they took with them like Agent Orange and drug addictions. Some of my classmates returned via Dover Air Force Base with six people carrying their remains for their much too early final resting place. Others picked up their lives. I see them at some of our annual events. Thank you for serving because freedom is not free.

I was college bound because of my achievements in the class room and by the grace of one of the best basketball programs in this country. My father had made it very clear, that as part of the American Dream, I had to go to college. Dad also denoted that as the third child of seven with two sisters in front of me college bound and two sisters following me college bound, I would be fully responsible for my college education and its expense, you are a man my son!

Our family could not be considered middle class, in any way, so we were the working poor, living from paycheck-to-paycheck. My father worked a second job so Catholic school could be had by his children. My dad believed that the only way to get equality was via an advanced education. Now basketball was making this dream possible. I now had to choose among thirteen schools that I had visited to consider my next step in my educational sojourn towards becoming a doctor. I should explain that between my junior and senior year in high school, I received over two hundred letters showing interest in me visiting their schools basketball program. Most of these letters did not get opened because the logo and team mascot would determine if you wanted to play in the Big 10, ACC or Ivy League.

During my junior year at DeMatha, my best buddy, Sid, wanted to convert to Catholicism and did so by taking my father's name, Ignatius, as his baptismal name. Sid and I did everything together from basketball to school proms. Sid was asked to go to Boston with the coach of the Boston Celtics, Mr. Red A., to make a high school basketball film. I was asked to be the stand-in dummy for Sid as he showed off his 6 foot 8 inch, 235 lb. moves for a new era in the "big-man" basketball. This is where and when the game of basketball went above the rim and not below. The set-shot was now going out and the jump-shot was coming in. The dunk-shot was coming into full bloom but would be short-lived because of these new seven-footers that were now coming into the high school and college arenas. Dunking the basketball for points would be taken out of the high school and college game for the next five years but only for a time. It would return later with a vengeance and a new generation of big, faster and stronger athletes.

Being a sought-after college recruit was an adventure for me. I knew that I was becoming a good basketball player but not a great basketball player. I knew my size at now over six feet six inches was good but not great. Therefore, I had inherited my dad's wisdom and followed his repeated advice: "A wise man knows and knows he knows; a fool thinks he knows, and knows not." Daddy would always remind me not to be a fool.

....If you can keep your head when all about you

Are losing theirs and blaming it on you;

If you can trust yourself when all men doubt you,

But make allowances for their doubting too....

IF – by Rudyard Kipling

UCLA was too far. Notre Dame (ND) was getting three of Washington, DC's top all-stars including my buddy, Sid. Sid would be joining our former teammate Bob W, who had blazed the trail to South Bend, Indiana, and now the Calvary from DC was on its way. I had the full scholarship offer in hand from ND but I know what I know and going to ND would make tough going for anybody like me. I had played with these four players and competed with them; and, in most cases, had beaten them if they were not part of the same team. I visited a number of schools in the southern United States like Davidson, Florida State, Maryland University and others. For many of these schools, I was going to be their first black basketball player. I had cycled through this process before. Being the first or only black basketball player was not a major concern of mine. Remember, my father had written my "Mission to Equality" at age seven when I made my first Holy Communion. I had it down pat by now. I was just as good as the next guy. If I applied myself in mind, heart and gut, I would win at any match to which I committed. This was just another piece in "The Flow of Life".

Well, now it is March of my senior year and I was forced to make a decision because time was running out. My father said that I had to take that next step. At the last basketball tournament of my senior

The Flow of Life

year in high school, I was now playing some of my best basketball of my short career. I made the All-Tournament Team and was the Outstanding Rebounder for the Knights of Columbus Tournament. This tournament brought in the best of the high schools from across the country. As Coach Frank would say in our private session after regular practice, I was playing above the rim where the game was supposed to be played. At one of the time-outs in the final game, Frank leaned over and said, "Eric, do you know where your head was on that last play?" I looked at him and smiled and said, "Where you said the game is played, above the rim." DeMatha was not the favorite going into this tournament because we had to face tough teams out of Philadelphia and Chicago. If we made it past them, we had to face a team that had beaten us twice in that same year where the number one scorer in DC/MD basketball lived. His name was Austin C.

I knew the uphill battle we as a team were facing. Austin was one of five players that I use to fit into my 1963, Gray VW. Yes, that's six people in a VW bug. I was the driver so my seat was safe. Sid's seat was safe because he was my best buddy. So there were three other spots and the stick seat. It wasn't a seat but a space around the stick in the floor. It was for Tom L. Tom had a jump shot of twenty-two feet long before the three-point shot came to be. I think Tom shot about a 60% rate at hitting his jumper from this range. Tom was allocated to the front seat because he was the smallest person in the car at 6 feet 2 inches.

The back seat had Collis J., at 6 feet 7 inches; in the middle slot was Austin Carr at 6 feet 4 inches; and, the other seat door-side was Ed E. at 6 feet 6 inches. All of us were adorned in huge Afro's which took up a large portion of the VW Bug in itself. The aha moment came in as bystanders witnessed all of us unloading the VW Bug, one lanky extremity at a time, until we escaped the confined tightness of the "cockpit". Only Carlos Jones had a high and tight haircut because of his affiliation with St. Johns Military Academy. There were four different schools represented in this VW: two catholic schools, Mackin and DeMatha; one public school, Cardoza High School; and one Catholic military school, St. Johns Military Academy. We would reach the location of one of several outdoor courts and ask for the next and would take on the winners. No doubt I was the sixth man, but these guys allowed me to run with the best of the best, the best mentor program in the world. Within two short years and a lot of jumping practice, I was able to keep pace and rise to the occasion above the rim.

Chapter Three

At the conclusion of that final high school basketball game, I was set. I was going to play in the Big 10. Coach Dave S. had been to my home and out to dinner several times, meeting my dad. He had also taken me to dinner several more times and talked with my father a hundred times. Also, I had visited the University of Michigan in the fall of my senior year. Coming out of the locker room, you were usually met by young fans requesting your autograph. I was approached by a guy that introduced himself as Dickey S. He said that he was there on behalf of St. Joseph's College in Philadelphia. I said that I had been to Philadelphia for a visit to Temple University, but I was heading to University of Michigan and that I was all set.

Dickey then said, "I understand you have a strong interest in becoming a doctor." I said, "Yes, that is true, and that's the reason I am heading to Michigan over some other schools that don't have Pre-Med Programs." Dickey then informed me that St. Joseph's played in the Big 5 and the school had one of the top Pre-Med programs on the east coast. Now Dickey had my attention. I asked how that was possible when less than half the people who apply to medical school got admitted. Dickey then stated that over 90% of the students who complete the Pre-Med Program gain admission to medical or dental school through the St. Joseph's program.

Well, I had to check out this story! Another week of delay for Michigan would not make a critical difference because my spot was there if I wanted to attend the University of Michigan. So, I took Dickey and St. Joseph's College up on their offer to visit their school and talk with admissions and the Pre-Med Program Director.

I can tell you that there were no frills on this recruiting trip. On the University of Pittsburgh trip, I stayed at the new Hyatt Regency Hotel and saw the Righteous Brothers in concert. At St Joseph's, I stayed in a resident dorm with no concerts. My name did not show up anywhere on campus as it had at the Maryland University where they made it "Welcome Eric Day" over the main entrance to the University off of US 1. St. Joseph's was the only trip in which I took the train as opposed to a plane. There were no concerts and no extras, just the facts and nothing more. Here are the facts. The pros were: St. Joseph's did have a great admission rate into medical school; St. Joe's was just a train ride from Washington, DC rather than a plane ride to Michigan with the expense to see me play for the family; St. Joe's was just a train ride home to visit, and I would drive it in two-and-a-half hours, not the twelve hours from the University of Michigan. I was only required to come out the first day of practice and try out. My scholarship would otherwise stay intact as long as I had passing grades. The cons were: I would be playing on a slightly smaller national stage. If I got injured at the University of Michigan, my scholarship could be at risk. The academic side of the Michigan campus was not linked like it was at St. Joe's. The biggest con at St. Joe's was that I could not be part of the Pre-Med Program until after a semester of courses was completed, with a C+ average.

The pros outweighed the cons. I selected St. Joe's as my next step in my plight to my long-term dream of becoming a doctor. Another pro that I brokered into my selection to come to Philly and not Michigan was that I could go to summer school every summer, complete with books, room, and board. The deal was struck, and I returned to Washington, DC to finish my senior year in high school.

The end of high school came quickly with graduation on the 4th of June. June 5th was a packing day and June 6th was the travel day. On June 7th, I checked into Sullivan Hall and signed up for two courses for both semesters of summer school. My dad and the old VW bus made the trip but without my basketball trophies that I had collected over the past two years. My father said, "You don't need those awards. The objective is to go and get new ones." My trophies stayed with him.

I had class every day and, to earn my meals, I worked on the maintenance crew for the college. I was paid in Horn-n-Harvest vouchers for the local restaurant on the corner of 54th and City Line Ave. My roommate was another basketball player named Bruce and he, too, was there taking a course for the summer. I explained to Bruce that I was trying to get ahead because I knew how much time basketball would take and I was going to be a Pre-Med major.

The school courses, the work schedule and, of course, the basketball went well. I played in a summer league in Narberth with Bruce and several other local players who had also committed to St Joe's. A loyal fan of the College would come and get Bruce and me and two other incoming freshmen. He carted us about to these games because none of us had transportation. This summer school jump was major good, because I got to learn everything about the campus and the school before my official first day of school on Sept. 6th.

….If you can trust yourself when all men doubt you….

IF – by Rudyard Kipling

On September 5th, I went to see Father Moore. Fr. Moore, head of admissions for St. Joseph's College, was the person who told me that I could not be admitted into my freshman class as a Pre-Med but could change my major to Pre-Med after I had completed a semester of courses with a C+ or better average. Once in Fr. Moore's office, I requested a change in my major, History, to Biology Pre-Med. Fr. Moore, once again, was quick to remind me that this was only possible after I had a semester of courses and a C+ or greater average. I was equally quick to pull from my backpack a copy of my St. Joseph's transcript with two semesters of course work in two courses carrying greater than a C+ average.

Fr. Moore acknowledged that I had fulfilled the requirement to change my major but advised me against such a move. This is where I injected my dad into the equation without his knowing it. I told Fr. Moore that my father always said, "Start the way you want to finish." I told Fr. Moore that tomorrow school would start and whether I passed, failed, or even withdrew; I wanted to start the way I planned to finish. Presto, I was now one of 120 Pre-Med enrollees in the Freshman Class of 250 students at St. Joseph College in Philadelphia, Pennsylvania. Yes, one-half of the freshman class had denoted their college major as Biology, Pre-Med. "Here we go!"

School started the next day and things ran downhill for some time. General chemistry was so tough. The chairman of the department kept pushing me and advised me to keep at it and I would get it if I didn't quit. Thank you, Dr. B. All the other courses were good and basketball got off to a good start. In those years, freshmen could not play on the varsity and had to play freshman-team ball.

The Flow of Life

I lived in Barry Hall with an aging priest and thirty-one guys. My room was at the top of the stairs on the second floor. My roommates were Gene, Andy, and Daniel. There was a TV in the living room. Girls were not allowed in the front door of the house. Yes, I was the only black in this house and the only black in all of the fourteen other houses that peppered the campus to provide the on-campus living arrangement. I was also the only black ball player on the freshman or varsity team. Yes, I was an Island again but understood who I was, just like them!

I didn't have time to complain because I was very busy. I did not make it home for Thanksgiving or Christmas that year, or any year, because it was the basketball season. The schedule didn't permit time to travel to Washington, DC. My mother thought the coach had no heart because of this. My father would make the trip up to St Joseph's to see me play. He would bring my high school girl friend on occasion. The long-distance girlfriend didn't last long.

….If you can meet with triumph and disaster

And treat those two imposters just the same….

Rudyard Kipling

At the end of the first semester, I said to myself, "Houston, we have a problem." I had gotten a D+ in Chemistry, the first since fifth grade. Well, the Chairman of Chemistry said to keep pushing and not quit. The second semester started. I went on to sign up for Chemistry 2 for the second semester. My teacher in Chemistry was someone new and he thought and said that I would not make it out of his class with anything less than an F. I thanked him and dropped the course. Otherwise, the semester went well. The first year of basketball was finished. I was again the leading rebounder for the freshman team. Now the question was, "How was I going to rebound from being down with Chemistry 2 still to be had? Chemistry 1 and Chemistry 2 took out a number of Pre-Meds in the first year. Now the question remained how was I going to rebound from needing to take and complete Chemistry 2? How was I going to recover from being recorded with a D+ in Chemistry 1, Chemistry 2 still to be taken with Chemistry 3 required to complete the Chemistry nightmare? Yes, Chemistry 1 and Chemistry 2 took out a number of Pre-Meds in the first year and I was on the fence. I was still hanging over the edge of the cliff which had already taken out, let's say, forty of those 120 Pre-Meds who had started just ten months before.

By course count, I was still ahead in my course work because of my first summer school session since graduating from high school. I was ready to apply this course of action again. I put in for my summer school courses as part of my deal to come to St Joe's. My summer school request was in place. I signed up for Chemistry 2 and Chemistry 3 for that summer. The shortcoming in this design was that Chemistry 3 was in first semester and Chemistry 2 in the second semester of summer school. That was okay with me. I just didn't want to waste the first part of summer not taking a course. So off to summer school I went. Chemistry 3, here I come! I walked not fifty yards down the halls of the chemistry building when my nightmare of a teacher from my second semester popped out into the hall and inquired as what I was doing in the chemistry building. I explained that I was taking a couple of science classes. Well, he hurried off, only to return with the Chairman of Chemistry. Dr. B. gave me a different and "glad to see you" greeting. We talked about basketball for a little. He congratulated me on a great past season.

Now it was time to get down to brass tacks. Dr. B asked me about my plans for the summer school. I told him the truth. I told him that if I wanted to continue to play basketball, I had to catch up on Chemistry 2 and I had to get ahead with Chemistry 3. Dr. B. reminded me of the numerical order of 1, 2, and 3. I told him that I believed that I could do this odd sequence, if permitted. Thanks to my lucky stars, he said okay to it.

I worked very hard that summer and got a B in Chemistry 3 and an A in Chemistry 2. I was back on track and was now almost a year ahead in course work as I waited for year two to start. I went home for a few days that spring for my sister's high-school graduation and reunited with Frances M from my Catholic grade school days.

I had not seen Frances in five years. During those five years, she had turned into a raving beauty. I couldn't believe my eyes! The thick glasses she wore were gone. Yes she was still that ultra-smart girl from eighth grade but now without the coke-bottle glasses. She now had the curves of a young woman which had me very interested. We started dating long distance. I used my dad's coming to the games as a transport mechanism.

My dad did not mind the favor, but my coach approached me and asked why it was necessary for her to come to the games. I saw the message that he was sending. Every other player had their girlfriend at the game, but my Irish girlfriend was a distraction. Frances and I talked. We didn't want to take on another mission when we both were committed to our professional aspirations. We drifted apart, and went in different directions. As a budding classical piano player, I can still hear her playing, just for me.

St. Joe's won the Big Five Basketball Championship that year and we went to the NCAA as one of thirty-two teams. We lost in the first round of the NCAA, but I had been where only a few teams ever get. The tough course my second year was called Chordate Morphologies. This was an anatomy course which was deemed one of the hardest courses in the Pre-Med Program. Like general chemistry had taken its toll on "X" number of Pre-Meds, this biology course was the hurdle for the second year.

The course was taught by the only female teacher in the school at the time. She was the wife of one of the other biology teachers. She was a very good-looking woman in the all-male school, like a Venus flytrap in nylons. She was also teaching the hardest Pre-Med course. If you didn't make it through Ms. N's course, you could forget about medical school. On October 15th, the first day of official basketball practice started. Along with making the team, there was a lot of travel involved when playing for a Division I basketball team.

This was the first balancing act as both a varsity basketball player and a St. Joseph's Pre-Med student. Most science courses were four credits which meant that there was a lab attached to the course and your grade. The lab was usually late in the afternoon at about the same time as the start of basketball practice. This was not good because the head coach of the basketball team would now be missing one of his players one lab day per week. There was little that he could say, however, because it was part of my course work and my purpose for being enrolled into the College.

The Flow of Life

My two life-savers for second year biology were Dave and Ed. Dave and Ed were two other biology Pre-Med students who lived next door to me in Barry Hall. In November, the basketball team would take to the road for away games. I would miss that lab and lecture because of going out of town. Dave and Ed would get me up to snuff, sharing their notes. I was glad that they were two of the smartest guys in the Pre-Med Program. For the lab portion, they would go with me to the anatomy lab and we would remove the wrap of my cat sample, the cadaver of Pre-Meds, and review the lesson that I had missed. Again, thanks go to Dave J and Ed W. I got a good grade out of the course which was as important as taking and passing the course. This biology course in our second year would take out a good number, about twenty, of those Pre-Med students who were "left on the beach" when they landed into general chemistry from the first year.

Now the second year was complete and I was still in the Pre-Med Program. My objective now was to get another science done because in your junior year, you have two sciences. I could not miss two days a week of practice or class and believe that I could survive. I would have to take a complete year of one of my third-year sciences. I picked Physics with another liberal arts class to make for another full semester of courses during the summer of my second year. My challenge for this summer was that Coach said there was no money in the budget for food and housing for me. I told the coach it was not a problem because if I did not go to summer school I would not be able to play the coming season.

"The Miracle on 54th Street" occurred and presto, the Most Improved Player, voted by coaches and players, my newest trophy, from my first year of varsity basketball had help the school find some food for this student wishing to continue on his sojourn into medicine. That summer I worked at the same residence, Loyola Hall, where all the priests who were the major cord of the teaching force at St Joseph's in those days lived on campus. I was to work in the kitchen with Sam, the cook, who had worked there for over thirty years. I worked with Sam about four hours a day, and ate the best that I had ever eaten in my life. I went from 195 pounds to 215 pounds for my junior year. What a training table for a school that months before didn't have money in their budget for me! "The Miracle on 54th and City Line", the college's location, had happened and had fattened me up for the coming season. I got A's in the liberal arts course that summer and B's in both terms of science.

Eric I. Mitchell is on a roll. As a side-bar, the 'I' in my name is for Ignatius, my father's and my grandfather's first name. As that pit bull Catholic, my father and mother chose Ignatius as my middle name, for baptism. My Mission to Equality had been confirmed by my walking in my respective place for First Holy Communion and not the back of the line.

St. Joseph's College was so embodied with the Founder of the Society of Jesus who was St. Ignatius of Loyola. St. Ignatius is my patron saint whose feast day is one day before my birthday. He was a Spanish knight from a local Basque noble family, hermit, priest since 1537, and theologian, who founded the Society of Jesus and, on 19 April 1541, became its first Superior General. Ignatius emerged as a religious leader during the Counter-Reformation. Loyola's devotion to the Catholic Church was characterized by absolute obedience to the Pope.

And to think that I did not want to go to Catholic high school and I did not want to go to a Catholic college. And here I was in the vortex!

Chapter Four

A sign of the time was upon us. Martin Luther King had visited St. Joseph's College about one year before he was killed in Tennessee. The enrollment of minority students had increased in the day student population, but I was still one of only blacks who lived on campus. The other minority was a tennis player from Jamaica who had enrolled at the start of my sophomore year and lived in one of the other house-dorms. We had a new dorm being built at the time as one of the major expansion projects for the school. It would be completed by the start of my junior year.

At the start of my junior (3rd) year, the largest class of minority and black students was accepted into the school. The number of blacks living on campus would increase five to six fold. A number of day students and the only minority students on campus formed a society called the Black Awareness Society. I was the major organizer of this because there were many first-time issues which would come up. I had learned from my father that sitting on these issues didn't often hatch the desired result. My father always said, "There are only two things you can do in life; you can act or re-act; and when you are reacting, it is because someone has already acted upon you or the situation at hand. So act!"

I am not sure how my name got to the Philadelphia Urban League (PUL), but the then director, Andy Freedman, came and visited me at St Joseph's, then College, now University. He asked if I would be willing to come for an interview. I said, interview for what. This interview would be for a seat on the Board of Directors for the Philadelphia Urban League. I accepted the invitation and was interviewed and accepted to become the first college student on the Board of Directors for the PUL in its history. I would spend the next twenty-five years with the PUL in some form of public service. As a result of my long commitment to the PUL, I was somehow voted and received the NAACP Outstanding Citizen Award for Philadelphia 1996.

My next academic objective would be Organic Chemistry, which would be the final hurdle in the Pre-Med course. Physics and Organics would take out maybe twenty more of the remaining sixty Pre-Meds. Being on the road playing basketball and studying organic chemistry made for a tough year, but I understood it was necessary because now we also had to start applications to medical schools. If you got an interview, you had to go and visit the medical school as the final step for acceptance.

There was a staff committee at St. Joseph's in those days that wrote a letter of recommendation for the medical schools that people applied for. I was informed midway through my junior year that the committee wasn't sure they were going to write me a letter. They decided that I didn't have a 3.5 or greater average and doubted a medical school would consider my application.

Interrupting this personal concern, a non-academic issue arose for the minority students and it had to be taken to the dean of students. The black students had been in different house-dorms spread over the campus. The majority of these minority students wanted to live together. I took the issue to the dean of students and got a section of the new dorm for the minority students. It would be called King Hall in honor of MLK. I advised the BAS member that I would continue to room with Danny as I had for the previous years and would continue to do so for my fourth and final year. Let it be told now, where the statute of limitations have surely expired, that Danny and I had the best room on campus in Barry Hall, and wild horses could not have pulled us away from each other or this room. We had a deck off our room, a private entrance; a semi-private bathroom; a jazz collection of Danny's which was second-to-none; and, a private parking space next to our room. Also, we had only one hundred feet or the thirty yards to the Field House.

I then met with the letter writing committee and listened to their concerns. I warned them that as a Division I basketball player and with a science average greater than a B average, I would go to the Philadelphia Urban League, NAACP and American Civil Liberties Union if my letter was not written. My letter was written. I put out a dozen applications to different medical schools in Boston, New York, Philadelphia, Washington, DC and Georgia.

George Washington University in Washington, DC was my first letter I received granting an interview. So I was now returning to my hometown for my first test of fire. The interview was considered a critical step in this process towards admission into medical school. No doubt, the members of the admission committee were looking for that fire in the belly. Well, I brought an inferno with me. Six weeks later, in the first week of September before the start of my fourth year at St Joe's, I got my first admission to medical school letter. My senior year had not yet started. I had been accepted into medical school for the next year's class starting September 1971. My final year's course work at St. Joseph's College would be of my choosing because I had all the credits plus that I needed to graduate by the end of my junior year. I had my senior year of basketball just ahead of me. This would mean that where would be no missed practices or labs in the future. There would be no critical make-up examinations after I returned from a missed class. Bring it! I would return to St Joseph's University fifteen years later as part of the President's Council and then the University's Board of Trustees.

Now, I was the only the second Division I basketball player in St. Joseph's history to get accepted into medical school. My junior year in basketball didn't bring the same division title but I had collected my second Most Improved Player award at the annual Sports Awards Dinner to add to my growing collection of trophies, some here in Philadelphia with me and those that my dad was in possession of in Washington DC.

The pressure was off with this early medical school acceptance, but I had another eleven applications out there. This was deja vu all over again like my high-school basketball trips to different schools all over the east coast. I would get more letters granting interviews from other medical schools and I would go. I got multiple acceptances into medical schools along the East Coast in Washington, DC, Philadelphia and Boston. There were forty-one biology Pre-Meds left out of the 120 who entered as such with me three year earlier. In the fall of our senior year, each day, someone would get a letter of acceptance to medical school and a slap on the back would be in order and the beat went on. 40/41 Pre-Meds would get into medical or dental school. So the percentages that I was posed with my Dickey S. four years earlier were holding. I was so glad to be among the 93% that got into a professional school of medicine or dentistry.

The Flow of Life

As I knew it, only about three or four of us in the remaining junior Pre-Med class put in applications to Ivy League medical schools, the three smart guys in our class and me. Two of us got interviews and two of us got accepted to one of those schools. Well, well, well, now what was I going to do? Go Ivy League, or not? This question was quickly answered and that was a yes to Go Ivy League. U of P or bust! The Medical School at U of P or Penn was the first medical school in the United States. I would be entering the 210th graduation class in its 206th year in existence —September, 1971.

We won our basketball division again my senior year. We were off to the NCAA again for the second time in three years. The results were no better, getting knocked out in the first round, but it was all good because the NBA was my distant second choice over medical school.

This choice became a little less distant and a little more difficult after I was awarded the Most Valuable Player (MVP) for the very first United States vs Philadelphia All-Star Liberty Bell Classic game. Now, this is where a disclaimer is needed. Two of the best basketball players in Philadelphia were not in the mix for this all-star game for Philadelphia. One great player was hurt and one was hiding out because he had signed a professional contract before the season had ended that made him illegal for collegiate participation. At the writing of this book, both of those players in all their college greatness have passed on in the flow of life. God Rest!

Four years had passed since leaving Washington, DC. When I selected St. Joseph's over University of Michigan, I knew that three of my closest buddies would be heading for Notre Dame. Now two of those three were back in Philly-town, and one of them was the NCAA scoring champion, Austin Carr. His NCAA record for scoring the highest point total for a single game would stand for thirty-plus years. Now, Austin was in Philly and we were reunited before, during, and after this All Star game.

Austin Carr would be the number-one draft pick for the NBA our senior year. Even forty years ago, this was a big event and would bring a contract then equal to a million dollars, but not the twenty million or forty million dollars as is true for today's number-one draft choice. Yet, a million dollar contract in those days was still big bananas and that person had some say in the organization. Austin invited me to come try out for the NBA team. He was soon headed for Cleveland, Ohio, as the number one pick in the draft that year. As inviting as this invitation was, I had been admitted to one of the top Ivy League medical schools in the United States of America and the first medical school in the country. I knew people who were leaving the United States for medical school outside the USA and abroad. No, I would bite down on the bit and pull in my ropes on my basketball ambitions.

There was no summer school this summer for graduation from college was done.

Chapter Five

When I got my diploma from St. Joe's, it came rolled up in a cardboard container. I didn't, and wouldn't, look at or open this degree until I completed medical school. I told myself that this degree was only a stepping stone to my goal. Yes, I was now the first in my family's history to complete college. My two older sisters were pending graduation. I knew that I had more work to do and didn't want to lose my perspective. I didn't believe any medical school was going to be easy, but I believed that I had picked one of the most difficult.

I had to move from St. Joe's and find an apartment, moving off campus and finding my way every day to the Perelman School of Medicine at the University of Pennsylvania. My girlfriend from the nearby Catholic girls' college was one year in the making from an introduction by one of my Hawk underclassmen. I wanted to be near where she lived so I got my first apartment in Germantown, Philadelphia. I had to pay for medical school, pay for my rent, pay my board, and all the rest. I knew better than to even ask the question back on the home front. In my four year in college, I have two more sisters who enter college. There were no scholarships to medical school as it had been for college with basketball. However, I had my tool bag which was the only thing that my dad let me bring with me from Maryland four years earlier. I had put these tools to good use in the summer and on weekends when free from basketball travel. They say that the fruit never falls too far from the tree.

....If you can wait and not be tired of waiting....

IF – by R. Kipling

I have to jump back in time, to about age nine. From age nine until I left for college, I worked every weekend when my dad was not working for the Post Office. We had a painting and remodeling business, called I. Mitchell and Son. At age nine, I helped my father build his sister a house which still stands today on Annapolis Road/ Route 450 Laurel, Maryland. I learned to paint, repair and build with dad. I was taught to mark twice, cut once. Dad's mantra would serve me well in the years to come as a building contractor, and later a surgeon. "Mark twice, cut once".

I had to put all of these talents into my first apartment because it was a handyman's repair special. It was not pretty for there were holes in the walls and doors falling off. However, the price was right so I patched the holes, hung the doors, painted the place and did window dressings. It worked well. I spent my first year of medical school in this apartment. I walked about ten blocks and caught the train from Germantown into Center City and to the medical school at 36 and Spruce Street.

The first day of class was about to start for medical school. The whole freshman class was assembled in the amphitheater for our introduction to the Perelman School of Medicine at the University of Pennsylvania, the first medical school in America, commissioned by Benjamin Franklin in 1765. There was a person that mounted the stage with a full-length white coat. When he moved across the stage, the white lab coat appeared to be stiff with starch, making his movement look somewhat robotic. After he took a minute or two to look over the amphitheater in silence, he announced, "You are a chosen few in these 140 seats". It is not possible to interview 15,000 applications so 1,200 applications were granted an interview to this Ivy League School of Medicine. Just over 10% of these interviewees would be selected to fill one of these 140 seats. Further, the white coat said that "You have been admitted to these halls and you will have rights that no other professional will have or will be granted."

….If you can trust yourself when all men doubt you,

But make allowance for their doubting too….

IF – by Rudyard Kipling

Well, from his first outcry of "You are a chosen few," I was looking around for who he was talking about. I looked about the room and I counted about ten black students, about ten women, and about a dozen Asians; the other 100 plus were white men. This distribution was not surprising to me. I saw some people so puffed up after listening to this guy, they had a problem getting out of the door because their heads were already too big for the door jam.

Our classes would start and anatomy and physiology would be the order for the next sixteen weeks. I made quick friends with people at my anatomy table and found a buddy who had played Lacrosse at a Division I level. We connected. Our class of eleven minority students was the largest number of black students ever admitted into a single class at Penn in its 200 plus year history. There was a national movement for colleges and universities to admit more minority students. There were only about ten other black students enrolled in the medical school that were scattered in the other three years of classes. I had been interviewed by one of them when I visited the medical school in the fall of my senior year of college. His name was Gregg and he was now in his senior year. I hooked up with him just to say thank you for the interview. He must had said, thought or wrote down some good things about me. He advised me that no man or woman was an island here and urged me to group up with somebody to study with ASAP.

This advice was taken right from the start and about six of us from our first-year group reviewed the material of the courses. We all spent a lot of time in the library doing study time. We all had an advisor who was no one other than a faculty member to talk to and tell us where to find stuff which was important.

There were soon two emerging potholes in the road with the first being a designation by someone in the medical university that they were going to release the grades of just the black students' admitting class for our group admitted in September.

When this breach of privacy was proposed, we the freshman students went to the Dean of Minority Affairs. This professor of Ob-Gyn had been in this fight with the University since she was a resident at the University forty years earlier. She got us a meeting with the Dean of the Medical School. We convinced the Dean that nothing good could come out of releasing just the black student data. My suggestion in that meeting was to include all students or none of the students. My sojourn as a board of director member with the Philadelphia Urban League was now five years running and I had learned a little about the power of diplomacy.

The Flow of Life

Things were going well with the weekly tests in these two courses. On the final, I aced anatomy and failed physiology. The physiology final was an essay type test. I didn't make the grade. There were no retests. I was in a proverbial hole again. I was told that my only option was to retake it next year. Ok, I had to worry about this later. I had my second-semester courses to worry about and clinicals would be starting. There was a short course during the break between the two semesters in both the winter and the summer sessions. I took additional mid-semester courses every year for all three years and passed them.

Was that just a pothole in his road to becoming a medical doctor or would that be a sink-hole where the road would be washed out to his doctoral dream?

….If you can dream—and not make dreams your master;

If you can think—and not make thoughts your aim….

IF – by Rudyard Kipling

Chapter Six

The second semester of medical school was micropharmacology and the start of clinicals. There were tests and more tests but no essay-type test that tested my writing ability like physiology had. I have had a spelling problem going back to the first grade and I always thought it was the fact that I had never learned my phonics or something like that. The start of clinicals was great. I liked the interaction with the patients.

I used the library as my study station so other things would not pull on me if I left school and returned to Germantown. There was still basketball because I had to have exercise in order to keep my brain going. Miles, my lacrosse buddy, would always be ready for a game or two. There was a Penn intermural basketball league. We found enough people and ringers to put together a winning team.

....If you can talk with crowds and keep your virtue,

Or walk with Kings—nor lose the common touch....

IF – by Rudyard Kipling

In that winter of January, 1972 there was a heat wave. The temperature outside reached into eighty degrees. I was in the library trying to study with a temperature outside the library of about 84 degrees, and the temperature inside the library about 94 degrees. Study was impossible. I didn't want to start my trip home this early for it was just getting dark. In our first several weeks of clinicals, an invitation was extended to the first year students that we could always observe in the local ER, but we were not to get in the way. So I put on my short white coat and headed through the gate right next to the library to the ER of Philadelphia General Hospital (PGH).

PGH had a long, long history in Philadelphia. The point of this night was to see what was going on in the ER of this, at one time, 1200-bed hospital. I found that I was not the only student there in the ER doing observation. There were about thirteen or fourteen curtained bays where people were in different stages of receiving care. The waiting room was full and there were sirens arriving with a frequency that kept things jumping. I made it down to bay number eleven where a spotlight illuminated a hole in the large green drape that was placed over the head of a young woman. Inside the drape was a large laceration that extended all the way along the side of her face. The bleeding had been stopped and the wound draped out. There were two white coats at the examination table overlooking this patient's wound. The young person in the white coat had instruments in hand and was following some instructions of the older white coat lead person. His jacket said Dr. "Somebody".

....If you can keep your head when all about you

Are losing theirs....

IF – by R. Kipling

I looked on with great interest and could see the frustration in the face of the younger man in a white coat. His hands did not like the instruments in his hands or vice versa. The doctor asked him why he was here. The young man in the white coat responded that it was because he had to be, but the lab was where he really wanted to be. With that, the doctor took the instruments from the man's hand, and asked him to leave. The doctor followed the young white coat out of the bay and his eyes fell on me. He looked up and asked, "You came to do this?" There was no hesitation in my "yes, doctor." I had listened to his instructions to the now vanished white coat and now I had the stage—a cover over a face I had never seen, a hole in a face, surrounded with green drapes.

….If you can fill the unforgiving minute

With sixty seconds worth of distance run….

IF – by R. Kipling

One of the first things a first-year medical student does when they get to medical school is start practicing tying sutures. Well, I had been no exception to this rule and had my one-hand and two-hand ties down pat. Now was the time to put all that practice into application on this hot winter night. I jumped in, pulled on my white coat, washed my hands, and gloved up. I could tell the doctor liked my actions. I had to pull up a chair because I was tall and the table was too low. The doctor pointed out where I should start and directed me to bisect and bisect until I got the wound closed.

About forty-five minutes later, I met the young woman under the drape. Domestic violence actions had struck her in the face with a pickaxe, doing the damage. The eye, nose, and mouth were not involved so it was a straight plastic case from an ER standpoint. The doctor turned to her and told her how to care for the wound, what

The Flow of Life

problems to look for and to return to the "plastic" clinic in four days. An appointment was given to her. The doctor turned to me and told me I should try to follow this patient and that I should remove about one-half of the sutures every four days.

I had to find the "plastic clinic" for this city hospital and determine when this patient would return. I followed this patient until I had removed all her sutures. I got to see my final result which looked good for a bad situation. From that point on in my medical school career, I would spend every Thursday PM in the ER for about four to six hours in the evenings after school for the next two-and-one-half years. I was soon to be considered a regular and given duties far beyond observation. This was the best on-the-job training one could ask for.

Year one would come to completion with no additional damage. There were elective courses that could be taken during the summer with no additional cost. Tuition was from September to September so I thought why would I not use June, July, and August? I had always used the summer as a get-ahead time. Medical school would be no exception. The summer passed with a couple of courses and a rehab construction job for a Formal Company near my old college. I had done painting and building of showrooms for this owner during my time in college. He was about to open a new store and wanted me to do it. I got the job and would take my pay in a monthly allocation which would get me through the next eight to ten months of food and rent.

Now, I needed to find another apartment because my next-door neighbor was running an age-old profession as "lady of the night". Her front door should have been a turnstile and it would have been more effective. I was offered services but clearly rejected her offer.

41

I was able to find an apartment about five blocks away on the west side of Penn Street. It was a move up, to the west side. Germantown Avenue was like a line of demarcation from poor to the next step up. I even found a little old lady across the street from my new apartment that needed my handyman skill and services.

Chapter Seven

My second year was about to start. I had to see how I would be going to deal with Physiology again. I had a plan. I met with the Dean of the Medical School and the head of the Department of Physiology, Dr. F. Even from a weakened position, I wanted to act and not react to this repeat physiology position. So I made my request to the dean that I needed to repeat Physiology under the watchful eye and tutelage of the Department Chairman, and I requested to be in the class of the Chairman. The Chairman of the Department, Dr. F, reacting to my introductory statement, committed a major faux-pas and blurted out that I knew too much and did not need to be in his class. My response to Dr. F's statement was that I now just needed to put it into a format that would allow me to pass the course and that I would depend on him to be that guiding light. There was then a bequest of Dr. F. that I have additional help which would occupy another block of time and put me behind schedule. I expressed to the Dean that I believed that I could pass this course without any additional demand on my time since I had worked hard on my essay skill and I had passed all my other courses I had taken to reach my second year of medical school. The Dean agreed to the plan and now I had to just do it.

My second year would start with Physiology and Dr. F. Now, I had to fill my other time slot with something that would hold my interest and get me credits toward my degree. I applied and got accepted into an orthopedic research program for that semester. I met with the Chairman of Research, Dr. B. He asked me what I would like to do and I told him that I had heard about the electrical bone work he was doing here at Penn. Dr. B. laughed and said that the electric bone projects were not for students rather they were for the research residents. I would select and study the Ring of Ravia which would be another life changing event. However, it would be almost three years later before I would understand the second order effect of this course, and my decision to take it when I did.

Physiology was done by Christmas and I was back on course and Physiology and Dr. F. was a bump in the road, gone by. My research in the Department of Orthopaedics helped me keep pace and on course to my MD degree. Large numbers of minority students around the country had not made it past their first year of medical school. We still had all of our class enrolled. I was glad that I was part of this group. Two years in and another Christmas session with a summer session to follow put me ahead of my schedule for graduation. Midway through my second year, clinicals were in full force. I first took my orthopedic courses to make sure that I wanted to follow this course of action. I was all in. I took my sports medicine course with the doctor of the Philadelphia Eagles and knew this would be my mission. Another early elective course was surgery. At this point in time, I am now about one year of weekly ER encounters in, and I was never very withdrawn or shy so I am just looking for opportunities to get my hands dirty with each clinical course. My Leo nature is leaking from my pores.

I enjoyed all kinds of surgery on this rotation. An older orthopedic surgeon needed help one day for a procedure that he was about to attempt. Yes, attempt, because this procedure had never been done at the Hospital of University of Pennsylvania (HUP). However, this procedure had been done many times overseas and around the world

The Flow of Life

but had not hit the shores of America. The instruments we were going to use were not new. In fact, this instrument was about thirteen years old. The surgeon was Dr. JJJ III (Dr. J.) who was sometimes defined as the "nutty professor" with spiked white hair all over his head with crazy ideas coming from the cortex below.

Well, I joined the "nutty professor" that day in the OR to lend him a hand with what I was not yet sure of. The instrument that Dr. J. had was a 1959 Watanabe 11 mm arthroscope. This was all new to me as well as all the other surgeons looking on. Spectators were peering through the port-hole windows of the operating room. Most of the senior staff looked on and thought Dr. J. had "lost his last marble". They came to the window, looked in, laughed and moved on.

I was helping Dr. J. do the first arthroscopic exam of a knee ever done at HUP. The scope was placed into the knee. The light source was tungsten light at the tip of the scope; the diameter of the scope was 11 mm. It was hard for me to see anything, but Dr. J. was seeing what he was hoping to see. He was injecting a lot of water into the joint in order to get some distension of the joint. We were looking inside the knee joint at the cartilage, ligaments, and menisci of this knee. We were also soaking wet with all the water needed for the procedure.

Prior to this event on this day, the only way to get a determination of the condition of the meniscus he was injecting a lot of water into the joint in order to get some distension of the joint. We were looking inside the knee joint at the cartilage, ligaments, and menisci of this knee. We were also soaking wet with all the water need for the procedures.

Prior to this event on this day, the only way to get a determination of the condition of the meniscus inside of a knee was by a radiological study known as an arthrogram. This is where radiopaque dye was injected into the knee area and then x-ray pictures were taken to look at the contour of the meniscus for possible tears.

The flow of the water in and out of that knee on that day had our surgical gowns wet up to our knees, but what happened on that day was bigger than anyone would imagine realize for some time. After those introductory surgical courses, I knew my direction and I was "ALL IN". I would now do my medical courses as a matter of getting them done. My dye had been cast at the surgical arena.

I was still engaged in my weekly ER work and by this time, they were looking for me by 5:00 p.m. every Thursday. I would take care of a lot of different patients and most of the people who had lacerations. I was increasing my skills and enjoying helping people.

Of all the staff in the ER, it is the nurses who made this engine run with top speed. In short order I know who to ask if help was needed and where. Once they saw my abilities to do a procedure or solve a problem they were my best advocates. I even won over the good will of one of the night nurse supervisors, Ms. S. Ms. S. was old school. She did not wear pants or scrubs only her white nursing uniform and, yes, a white nurse's hat. I did not think even then, there was another nurse in the hospital that wore their nursing hat. She made me part of the staff and let me gain entry to the café at night to get food and snacks. Thank you, Ms. S., for making me part and parcel to that night shift in the ER.

Chapter Eight

By the end of my second year and the start of my third year, I was now determined to be a leader. I was soon asked to be on the Admissions Committee for the School of Medicine of the University of Pennsylvania.

My clinical days went well. I pushed into my third year well ahead of schedule. Life outside of medical school had me move in my junior year into town only blocks from the hospital and medical school. This was because my girlfriend's uncle had an apartment over his office. The price was right and close to my growing clinical obligations for my rotations. This move would save me about two-and-a-half hours a day in travel time on the train into town and the walk from station to my apartment. There was no more on campus classwork and one may not see the medical school for weeks at a time unless you needed to see someone there or meet with your adviser.

There was no more classwork and one may not see the medical school for weeks unless you needed to see someone there.

By this time, I was the president of the Student National Medical Association (SNMA). The SNMA was the student branch of the National Medical Association (NMA). The NMA was an organization which was started when minority doctors were not able to join the American Medical Association (AMA). The times were changing, but the NMA and the SNMA grew more important as there were still many issues which needed to be addressed at these two systems developed into one America. There were now larger numbers of minorities in non-black medical schools for the first time in the history of American medical schools. There was also a change in the number of traditional black medical schools during this time, admitting white students in larger numbers to their ranks. Residency programs that had never admitted blacks in their history were opening their post-doctoral programs to minority students. Here is a short history of three people that made this all possible for me.

In my second year of medical school, I join the D. Hayes Agnew Surgical Society. This was one if not the oldest surgical societies in the country. Dr. Agnew was a surgeon on staff at Pennsylvania Hospital in the late 19th century. D. Hayes Agnew (1818 -1892) was the first John Rhea Barton Professor of Surgery at the University of Pennsylvania from 1878 to 1889.

The Agnew Surgical Society is the oldest student run medical student society in the country, founded in 1888 as a surgical interest group. Today, the goal of the Agnew Surgical Society is to serve as a link between surgical faculty and medical students and to promote medical student interest in surgical careers. I had the honor of being the president of this student surgical society for two years. The Thomas Eakins portrait of Dr. Agnew is world famous and was commissioned by surgical medical students in 1889 to honor Dr. Agnew.

It was Dr. Agnew who helped the first black graduate from Penn's MD program to get post-doctoral training when no other sources were open. That first graduate was Nathan Francis Mossell, MD. After graduating from Lincoln University in Pennsylvania, Nathan Mossell entered the Medical School of the University of

Pennsylvania. At Penn, he took second honors in his medical school class. After graduating in 1882, he became the most prominent of Penn's first African American students. Upon graduating, Dr. Mossell was trained first by Dr. D. Hayes Agnew in the Out-Patient Surgical Clinic of the University Hospital. Because of the difficulties blacks then encountered in securing internships in this country, Dr. Mossell then traveled to England to complete an internship at the Guy's, Queens College and St. Thomas hospitals in London. In 1888, after his return to Philadelphia, Dr. Mossell was elected (after overcoming significant opposition on the basis of his race) to membership in the Philadelphia County Medical Society, making him the first African American physician to achieve this honor.

There is a second person who also blazed a trail made possible for those to follow. This person was Dr. Helen Dickens. An Ohio native, Helen Octavia Dickens (1909-2001) was the only African-American female to graduate from the University of Illinois School of Medicine and later became the first African- American woman to serve in Penn's Department of Obstetrics and Gynecology. She is also recognized for being the first black person to receive the Gimbel Philadelphia Award (1971) for her "Outstanding Service to Humanity." By 1969, she was Associate Dean in the Office for Minority Affairs at the University of Pennsylvania and within five years had increased minority enrollment from three students to sixty-four. I arrived in 1971 as part of the largest class of minority students ever in the history of the University up to that time. Thank you, Dr. Dickens.

Midway through your third year you need to do two things—apply for a matching program for your internship year and try to find a residency program for your post-doctorate studies. The internship year was usually a surgical internship or a medical internship and, in some rare cases, a third type which included both. This third type, not a very common one, was called a rotating internship. I now had a bigger problem because I would have thirty course credits by the end of my junior year. I only needed thirty-one credits to graduate. Do I stay or do I go!

I had to pay for my fourth year of medical school, but if I could get that last credit in the summer between my junior and senior year, I would be finished before September of my senior year. I could graduate without commencement and have no internship to go to. I knew what I should do. Get help for this dilemma. I went to the head of the person who had oversight of the ER at Penn. I explained my situation of being one credit short of graduating in May of my junior year. Dr. M. looked over the two-and-one-half years of my weekly work in the ER, and determined that it fulfilled all the requirements for an independent study course. He granted me not one but two course credits. One problem down, one problem to go!

Now with this task out of the way, I started looking for an internship program because I had not enrolled into the matching program. However, once the matching program was announced, programs would start back-filling any open slots. I didn't have to go far or look far. The place where I sutured my first patient on that warm January night was right through the fence of the medical school. It was not the highest-profile internship program because it was an inner-city hospital with a lot of poor people and the hospital had passed its heyday, but it was still packed with a lot of pathology. I went to talk with Dr. C., who was the head of the internship program for Philadelphia General Hospital (PGH). Dr. C. was also a Professor of Medicine at Penn with additional duties at PGH.

Dr. C. said that if I wanted an internship spot, then I could have it. Wow! I have all my credits for medical school graduation and I have an internship. I have a girlfriend who said that she would marry me. We planned and got married three months before I graduated from medical school. Graduation was next. Graduation day from the first medical school in this country brought some interesting reactions which would stretch back over my three-year sojourn.

….If neither foes nor loving friends can hurt you;

If all men count with you, but none too much….

IF – by R. Kipling

My father was aglow that graduation day with my young bride and other friends and family in attendance. I would become the very first in our family's history to graduate with a doctorate in medicine, an MD to follow the Mitchell name. There were other people there in dismay. Dr. F. from the Department of Physiology was one. He wanted to know what I was doing at this graduation exercise in cap and gown. He knew that he had information that very few people had of my first year's shortcoming and now how could this be! There was an anatomy professor from my first year who vowed to me, one day in the lab that I would never get out of this medical school. I was glad that both of these people, and maybe others, could see the colors in my doctorate robe blowing in the wind. I didn't tell anyone that I was going to graduate at the end of my junior year, because "loose lips sink ships", and I needed to keep afloat for my next mission.

There was no time to celebrate, but I did go home and pull out my degree from St. Joseph's College and take a look at it. It had been three years since I had received it and I had never taken it from the cardboard tube. I wanted to see if my name was really on it. It was!

Several months before my graduation, not only did I get married, but I also got a phone call from a niece of the cat lady across the street from my second apartment. She validated that I was the guy that she was looking for. She then informed me that her aunt had died several months before. I extended my condolences and asked how I might help. The niece stated that I was the only person that her aunt would talk about and the family wanted to sell the house and wanted to know if I wanted to buy it. Buy the House? I had worked all around this house repairing this and that. It was a nice house, but I didn't have any money to buy a house.

I knew that I would be an intern at Philadelphia General Hospital (PGH) come June and my bride and I would need a place to live. The apartment over her uncle's doctor office was very small. So I talked to my dad who didn't have the money but suggested that I talk to his sister, who was my godmother. The price of the house was going to be $13,400. Twenty percent was necessary and my aunt thought it was a great idea. She agreed to lend me the necessary money.

I closed on the house and had to get it cleaned up and painted before my internship was to start. I called the president of I. Mitchell and Sons and asked how much would the toll be for him to come to Philadelphia and help one of those sons with a paint job. He laughed on the phone and said it would cost me nothing, but I would have to feed him. I asked him to bring five-gallon pails of paint from the paint store where we had bought all of our paint over the years. It was not long before that old VW bus pulled up in front of my new house with dad behind the wheel with a burned out Tiparillo cigar stuck in

The Flow of Life

the corner of his mouth stating, "Let's go to work, son." And work we did. The house got a good going over and it was ready for living.

I did feed the old man. I could see the pride on his face. We were sitting at the dinner table when I started humming at the table, which had always been a "no, no" in his house. When his response was no humming at the table, I looked up and smiled at him and retorted, "This is my damn table." We both laughed because he understood that I had set him up and had waited for a long time for that one. And he had taken it, hook, line and sinker. Thanks, dad!

….If you can force your heart and nerve and sinew

To serve your turn long after they are gone,

And so hold on when there is nothing in you

Except the Will which says to them: "Hold on"….

IF – by R. Kipling

Chapter Nine

The "Flow of Life" continued with my internship year. In the first year, post-doctoral, twenty-five interns were gathered together but that day no one told us we were the chosen few as had occurred on the first day of medical school. We were twenty-five your doctors from twenty or more different medical schools from across this country. We were given white pants and a white Ben Casey smock with our name on them. It had gone out of style in the 60s but was still part of the uniform for PGH in the 70s. I would be the only intern of the twenty-five interns that would wear my complete uniform with my black crepe-sole shoes that gave me another inch of lift and could get me through an eighteen-hour day on my feet. Remember, PGH had passed its heyday so the interns who had gotten here would consider PGH their second choice. For me, it was my first choice. I knew the value of the services that this hospital gave to this community. I lived seven blocks away. It also got me out of medical school a year early; it kept me in Philadelphia; and, I knew my way around the place all of the great pathology that still came to this city hospital. Good choice, Mitchell!

PGH still had a rotating Internship which meant I would be on different services: Pediatrics, Med/Surgery, ER and ICU several months at a time. I liked this format and went to it without any preconceived opinions. Pediatrics was my first rotation and this was all good because it was also close to the ER where I would hang-out when not busy with pediatrics and because they always had something going on in the ER. There was a brand new pediatrics hospital called The Children's Hospital (CHOP) of the University of Pennsylvania. I would also spend some time there because we would transfer some of our complex patients there as the hospital was just opening.

I denoted earlier that this was a city hospital which was one of the largest in its day in the United States. The hospital ran from 34th street on Civic Center Boulevard to 39th and Woodland Avenue. This was five full city blocks with the city morgue and the Mills building for mental health inpatients and outpatients at the 39th Street end. The city's drug rehabilitation program was also located in this building at about 38th Street. The main hallway was so long that you could not see from one end to the other. Most of my activities were at the 34th Street end of the building where Pediatrics, the ER, and the ICU were located. Police and Fire had a section of the building at about 36th Street junction where the police and fire members received their care from an outpatient and inpatient standpoint. The city's hospital detention center for injured and sick prisoners was also located in PGH where they received care. So PGH was many things for many people.

My bride had graduated from college and was now enrolled in a Master's program for reading also at the University of Pennsylvania. She was too afraid to stay at the new house when I was on call, but her mom and dad lived only four miles away where she could stay. I am sure that I worked too hard but I was doing the thing that I had longed to do for so many years, helping people get better. I explained to my bride that this was necessary if I was going to get to where I wanted to go. She said that she understood. And, I hoped so! You had to apply to get into a residency program almost before you graduated from medical school because of supply and demand. There were some programs that had a two to three year waiting list. From my basketball days to my first course elective in sports medicine, I knew what I wanted—an orthopedic program somewhere, somehow.

I applied to multiple orthopedic programs inside the city of Philadelphia and outside the city with fingers and toes crossed. I got an interview back through the gate at Penn's orthopedic program. Now, I interviewed with one of the professors, whom I did research with in my second year in orthopedics Dr. B. You can see here a second order effect being greater than a first-order effect from that little bit of research done during my second year of medical school while I was filling the Physiology hole that I had fallen into in year one. Everything happens for a reason.

My intern year continued to grind on. By now, I knew all the doctors in the Penn surgical residency program from my medical student ER days. Now many of those same doctors were senior residents within my internship program at PGH. The University of Pennsylvania ran the majority of the programs at PGH like Dr. C., who was a professor of medicine at (HUP). Several other medical schools in Philadelphia also had services which were run out of PGH.

Most of the senior surgical residents who rotated through PGH were headed for the plastic surgery fellowship programs across the USA. This concept of doing a fellowship after a residency was just coming into vogue. I was a benefactor of this developing trend. I was blessed with my physical presence of being over 6 feet 6 inches and willing and able to get in your face if you wanted to go there. Therefore, the normal banter, which is normally associated with a pecking order, was not there for me. I was given, allowed, and asked to take surgical cases which an intern would have never had an opportunity to do prior to this above trend.

The Flow of Life

In my rotation in ob-gyn, I did most, if not all, of the deliveries that were done during my rotational time on service. In orthopedic rotation, I got to do some cases even though the Hahnemann Hospital orthopedic program controlled the orthopedics at PGH at that time. My ICU rotation of two months was a lifesaver in several ways. The nurses in the ICU were my big teachers and I was their big student. This was where I learned to understand the dedication that these nurses put into their work had a direct relationship with who came out of that ICU alive.

My surgical rotation was also two months, but it really extended over my whole rotating internship year. Because of my relationships with the surgical residents through my ER work and my other rotations that I took as part of my core training, I became everyone's go-to guy. I was called upon from the other side of the back gate, the HUP side, many times over. In answer to their calls for help, whenever I could answer, I would.

My reward was the fact that I did over 150 major cases during my internship year. This was unheard of for an intern. Think guys! Oh, I say guys because at that time there was one woman in the surgical program that I knew of. It did not matter which rotation I was on. If there was a trauma in the ER, I would be STAT paged. A STAT page in those days was an overhead voice page. We had a beeper that just beeped and gave you a number to call.

My real two months scheduled in the ER was like old home week because I had now been coming to this ER for three-and-a-half years. This was the ER where it all started for me on that warm January night when the library was too hot and the PGH ER was hotter. I could usually anticipate an INCOMING, when I heard the siren coming out of West Philadelphia. The siren would grow louder as the police paddy wagon or the ambulance would turn onto Civic Center Boulevard for the five-block run down the Boulevard, to the ER entrance at the 34th-Street end of Civic Center Boulevard.

I was often the first-line of the surgical personnel to evaluate the stab or gunshot wound (GSW) in the ER. Whether or not I was in rotation or out of rotation, it did not matter. The ER staff was great and well trained, but they could be quickly overwhelmed with a highway accident or a gang fight breakout in West Philly. We would have a GSW come in and almost knew that there would be a possible second rebuttal GSW coming sometime soon after the arrival of the first GSW.

The most important part of these encounters was to stop the bleeding and start pumping in fluids and type and cross for blood. Dropping in a line in a trauma situation was to place a large bore catheter into the subclavian vein. This was done just above the clavicle and lateral to the neck. It was a blind stick and you would quickly know if you had it if you got a blood return. If you missed, you could get the apex of the lung causing a pneumothorax and then you would have a second problem to contend with in the treatment of the dying patient.

I was blessed in this regard because I had a great first time success rate in dropping in subclavian lines. There was a lot to be had. With that in mind, I will tell you a true story of one STAT page that I got for the Mills Building snack bar. Yes, the page came blasting over the loud speaker, "Dr. Mitchell, STAT, Mills Building, snack bar; Dr. Mitchell, STAT, Mills Building, snack bar. It was about 4:00 p.m. and I was at the 34th Street end of the complex. I was listening in some

The Flow of Life

disbelief when now my beeper went off and I looked at it and knew that the overhead page was real. It was not my pizza that was ready. In full whites and black crepe-sole shoes, I took off. I turned into the main hallway for a full five-block run. I was pretty fast and ate up the city blocks in short order. I turned the corner into the Mills Building with the snack shop straight ahead. There were people gathered. I asked for people to clear the way. I used my father's 1st Sgt.'s voice, with the bass so low vibrations rippled through the air. The sea of people parted and there, in front of the counter of the snack bar, was a pregnant woman on the floor with a bullet wound in the middle of her chest.

I saw that an emergency cart was being wheeled toward me. I asked who shot this woman. The cashier said, "I did." This behavioral health patient had received this GSW because she broke all the rules, and the seven inch knife beside her body got her a bullet in the chest. I was able to drop in a subclavian and get her to a location where I was able to put in a chest tube. This was to get her lung back up. The bullet missed the baby and the patient's heart. Both mother and baby were out of the hospital in four to five days to address assault charges along with her continued drug addiction and the delivery of a poor baby that would shake its way into a very scary world of withdrawal.

I did my time on the Police and Fire ward and met one of my lifetime friends named G. Mitchell. G. was about five years older than I and became my big brother of Philadelphia. G. was one of Philadelphia's finest and had been kicked by his horse. G. had a fracture of his patella. So I got to follow his progress and care. We have never been more than a phone call away for the past forty years in helping me out, whenever, wherever.

Chapter Ten

My intern year was coming to a close. It was a year for the records. I would soon be walking back through the gates to the HUP side of the fence. On the HUP side of the fence, I would be a first-year resident in orthopedics. The first year in HUPs program was a research year. There would be six residents in my year. On the first day, we met with the head of research. It was the first-time meeting for all the new residents except for me. For me, I had worked for this chairman of research in my second year on the Ring of Ravia study. I had also interviewed with this professor as well. So for me, this was my third-time encounter with Dr. B.

It was selection time for different research projects. I was quick on the draw to ask for the electric bone project. This time I got the research project without any discussion. It was hard to believe that three years had gone by. I now had a research project that was about to change the world of orthopedics.

I took up where the last first-year orthopedic resident left off. Some more clinical testing in our animal model was needed to determine the upper limit of the electrical anode charge that we wanted to put to bone to electrically stimulate bone growth. I got right to work. I met with the other members of the research team and fell into step. I had to implant New Zealand white rabbits with anode wires into their tibias with battery packs under their skin for six weeks. The tibias were then taken and slides were taken and stained for review of relative degree of bone growth per the anode charge. The upper and lower limits for bone growth were confirmed, and the clinical model for human implantation developed.

Dr. B. had a clinical Institutional Research Board (IRB) approval for implantation of these electrodes into clinical nonunions of long bones. The clinical objective was to implant this device into long bone fractures that were proven nonunion of fractures and heal them. A nonunion of a fracture occurs about five percent of the time in long bone fracture. At two million long bone fractures per year, this meant that there were about 100,000 nonunion of long bone fractures per year in the United States. The average nonunion would require 3.4 surgical operations at a very great expense to get them healed in full union. Therefore, we had a very large and willing population to draw from in the United States. HUP would receive a large number of these patients from across the country; and in some cases, from outside the United States, for a trial of this electrical bone stimulation to heal their osseous nonunion.

Now, Dr. B. has one of the largest nonunion bone clinics in the USA, if not the world. We are now implanting people with electrodes and following them with monthly x-rays.

Nine months have gone by and the Electric Bone Team puts together the results of our first seventy to eighty patients. The results look good so we submit this paper to the American Academy of Orthopedic Surgery (AAOS) for the annual winter meeting in New Orleans, LA. The paper was accepted for presentation at the AAOS.

I was selected to go to New Orleans and present this paper to the Academy. This was now surreal because most people in orthopedics can wait a lifetime to ever present to this academy and I was on my way to do so in my first year in orthopedics. Surreal!

....If you can make one heap of all your winnings

And risk it on one turn of pitch-and-toss....

IF – by R. Kipling

I got to the convention and was filled with excitement. I had checked and rechecked my research numbers. I was so ready to present and more ready for the onslaught of questions that would follow. All this work was ground-breaking at that time. Yet, I would not get my treasured chance to present to the Academy. From my mother, I received an urgent phone call saying my dad had been taken to the hospital and things looked bad. My dad has always been there for me and now I was going to be there for him.

I did not know what bad meant because I had limited information. I got some phone numbers from my mother who had been divorced from my father now for almost twenty years. I took the information and made my calls. My father appeared to have an aneurysm coming off the upper aorta. He was in a community hospital in Northwest Washington, DC. I talked with dad and he had some upper gastrointestinal upset for several days prior. He was taking his normal remedy of a pinch of baking soda, old school, but this time without relief.

The pain got worse and he was admitted because of severe hypertension and a preliminary study suggesting a dissecting aneurysm. I knew this was bad. We needed additional studies that could not be done at this community hospital to confirm the diagnosis (dx) and he needed to be somewhere where the surgery could be performed at the same setting. I flew out of New Orleans to Washington, DC that night. Dr. B. was at the Academy meeting and would present the paper for me. I had my dad to worry about now.

I flew out that night and into DC. I had dad transferred to one of the university hospitals. Studies were started the next day. The special test confirmed that surgery was very necessary to stop this dissection of this major vessel. Surgery was planned right away. The big need now was for blood for his surgery. All the brothers and sisters and the wives and husbands of our brothers and sisters were called to help. We all went together to the Red Cross center where twenty-two of us met and seventeen of us were able to give blood. So we had seventeen units of blood donated in the Ignatius Mitchell name. The ladies at the Red Cross were shocked when these twenty-plus people showed up at once.

The family migrated to the hospital to await the outcome of the surgery which was about to start. All that could be done was done from the family's standpoint. So we all wished dad good luck. He asked me how important this surgery was, being the only doctor in the family. I told him it was very necessary because he was bleeding inside. The dissection had to be stopped. My mother was even there. My dad's sense of humor was still intact. He told everybody that this was not a funeral wake.

Four hours later and still no word came from the surgical team. After hours five and six went by, I knew that things were not bright. At hour seven the surgeon came out and said they could not get him off the pump. There were some tears but the hours of him in surgery softened the seventh-hour news. All of his children were there. We all knew that there was more work to be done to celebrate his life.

Dad was going to get a twenty-one gun salute because of his military service. He would join several other family members in his final resting place. Taps were played for 1st Sgt. Ignatius Mitchell and the job was done. After a great repass, I planned my return to Philadelphia. It was time to get back to work. Dad would have wanted it that way, saying "keep your nose to the grindstone."

I had missed my opportunity to present to the Academy, but shortly after my return to Philadelphia I got a notice that Ebony Magazine, one of several magazines of Johnson Publication, Inc., wanted to do a feature article on me and the research that I was doing on electric bone healing.

Within a few weeks, a writer for Ebony magazine and a Pulitzer-Prize-winning photographer appeared and spent several days shooting pictures and writing the story. This magazine was a big hit with the family and was one for the scrapbook. This research resulted in one of the first human studies that we presented to the American Academy of Orthopaedic Surgeons. The resulting paper and papers from this research were accepted by leading orthopedic peer review journals. I also had my first publication. This publication would go into my professional curriculum vitae which is a scrapbook of a different type.

I finished my research year with multiple papers published on bone healing which would also become parts of textbooks into the future of medicine.

Chapter Eleven

I would now start my clinical rotation at different hospitals that Penn had a relationship with for our orthopedic residency. I started my clinical rotation at Pennsylvania Hospital which was the first hospital in the country founded by Dr. Thomas Bond and Benjamin Franklin. Pennsylvania Hospital also had one of the top orthopedic surgeons in the city, if not in the country.

Things got off to a good start. I fell into a great routine and knew all the answers for the situations. Things were right, dress right and I was ten, of the twelve, weeks into the rotation. In those days I was on-call every third day and night and the workday went for fourteen to eighteen hours. I left Pennsylvania Hospital on the night of August 18th for my twelve mile drive to my new home in the Germantown section of Philadelphia. Most of the ride was on the highway. I would get off on Fox Street, go down the hill, across Chelten Avenue, and would turn left onto Green Street to be home in five minutes.

....If you can meet with Triumph and Disaster....

IF – by R. Kipling

I did not make that turn on Green Street. I did not make it home that night. I did not make it home for the next nineteen nights. My 1968 VW met with a telephone pole and I was down and maybe out. This next part is all hearsay. Officer Brown of the Philadelphia Police Department was first on the scene. The car was totaled from the head-on impact. I was extracted from the car and transported to Women's Medical Center which was about three miles away. It took six people to hold me down to get an endotracheal tube down. I had disarticulated my face in what would be called a LeFort III facial fracture. I was hurt really badly. My left humerus was also fractured and there was trauma to my right ankle.

I am not sure how or who called the orthopedic staff at Pennsylvania Hospital, but in a short period of time the head of orthopedics from Pennsylvania Hospital was at Women's Hospital, barking orders along with his partner. His partner, Dr. M. at that time, was operational officer for the Pennsylvania Hospital orthopedic department. These two guys wanted me out of this hospital and wanted me at HUP where the only CAT scanner in the city was at the time. A pediatric ambulance was the only vehicle that Dr. M. could get at the time so he took it.

I was signed out Against Medical Advice (AMA) from Women's Hospital and was put in a pediatric ambulance with O2 and taken to the ER at Penn. In five years, I had gone from a student working weekly in this ER to now a patient in critical condition. The Chairman of Orthopedics at Pennsylvania Hospital had the Chairman of the Department of Neurosurgery standing by to take me to the CAT scanner to see the condition of my brain. I was comatose so all bets were off about my condition at that time.

The CAT scan was done and no major bleeds were found. I was placed in the ICU for respiratory ventilation and observation. My face was a mess. The best maxilofacial surgeon in the world would see me shortly after my arrival and determined that if I lived, I would need my face fixed. They did my facial reconstruction and how they did it

The Flow of Life

is unknown to me. I know that there were a lot of wires and buttons all over my face when I woke up thirteen days later. I was told that there were workers from the two hospitals, PGH and HUP, lined up one city block inside the hallways of HUP to see me and bring me their prays and best wishes.

Those first ten to twelve days were the most critical for me. I had one leg up because every nurse from the PGH ICU, through the fence, where I did my internship, took turns caring for me during that vital time. I was scheduled, by my understanding, that if I was not awake a trach tube would have to be inserted. Well, on day thirteen they were getting ready to start the set-up for the procedure. I told them not to touch me. Yes, I woke up and was trying to talk through my wires which held my mouth shut.

I made progress quickly once I woke up from the accident. I had my left humerus fixed with a plate and screws. This surgery was done with regional block and I got a small pnemothorax in the process of the anesthesia. I would write a clinical paper on this regional block anesthesia several years into the future with the same people that had done my regional block. I was now up and walking the halls of the hospital almost forty pounds lighter. I was transferred out of the ICU. They could not keep me in bed or in my room. I was not pretty to look at because I had facial buttons holding a very swollen face together. My brain was still wired together and now my teeth and jaws were as well.

My buttons and facial wires would stay in for eight weeks. My mouth was wired shut. My saving grace was a gap between my front two incisions, what I called the "Mitchell GAP". I would be released from the hospital five days after I woke up. My wife picked me up.

I insisted on driving home. My frontal and peripheral vision was intact; however, I had some central blindness in my left eye. I guess the left side of my face got the worst part of the trauma. I knocked out the alveolar ridge on the left as well as I blew out the left inferior orbital ridge. All these parts had been wired back into place. Thank you Dr. W.

I was now home in my little house with ice cream, tiger's milk and nowhere to go for this wandering tiger. In the thirteen days that I was down and out, I had lost about forty pounds. I did tiger milk and ice cream shakes about two to three times a day. There was nothing else that could get through that straw which fit so well between the "Mitchell GAP". Well, it worked because I gained back my weight and walked several miles every day. I even walked down to the accident scene to see the telephone pole that I had "bought" from the city.

After about ten more days of practice, talking with my mouth wired, I went to see the head of the residency program. I told him that I was ready to return to work. Dr. S. suggested that I take the year off and start my clinical over again next year. The next rotation had started in September and would run to December. I advised Dr. S. that I could teach the medical students for this next ten weeks and would be ready to go back to clinicals by January. This was the plan, and at about two weeks' post-hospital discharge, I was back in the hospital with my left arm still in a cast, my buttons on my face in place and my jaws wired shut.

It was not long before my buttons were pulled, my jaw wires released, and my left long-arm cast removed. Cocoa butter daily to the face did great things. Minus a loss of the left eye lid and some central loss of vision in the left eye, I was looking good and feeling great. I would not touch the left side of my face because of the paresthesia.

Now, I needed a car. A new VW was about all I would be able to afford, but I didn't want to put this big body back into a little VW. I knew somebody that knew somebody, who had an old Mercedes for sale that was in mint condition. I went to Maryland to see the car. It was beautiful and was built like a tank. It was a 1966 Dark Maroon 250 S MB. It was going to cost me $3,200 for this eleven year old car. I bought it. It would be my primary car for the next five years.

I taught the medical students, helped out where I could and was home every night for the next eight weeks. I started back with my next clinical rotation at the Hospital where I had been hospitalized. I had all the departmental eyes on me to see how I would respond to the work schedule and my duties in the operating room. I was back and I didn't miss a stroke. I was back and I asked for no special considerations.

Chapter Twelve

In keeping with my sports background and the fact that I was heading into sports medicine, like the first clinical school rotation, I went to see the head sports medicine orthopedic surgeon at HUP. He was Dr. S., and he was a big man with a great smile and white hair. I asked him if I could apply to be the orthopedic sports resident when I reached my senior year. Dr. S. said, "Why would you want to wait until you are a senior resident?" I said I thought it was a senior position. He said it was not but goes to the person that shows the most interest. From that day on until I graduated, I would be the orthopedic sports resident for the University of Pennsylvania sports teams and program.

This would mean that I would work with Dr. S. as the team doctor for all the University of Pennsylvania teams. This meant I helped to cover the football games, home and away. I would cover the track and field events, down to the world famous Penn Relays. One of those years, sprinter, L. James from Villanova University, set the world record for the 1/4 mile at 43.4 seconds. I would also take care of both home and away basketball when I could.

My next rotation would be very close to my home in Germantown because I would be returning to work with Dr. J.J.J. III again. I would be his only resident and I would get to play crazy with him. We played crazy together very well. Several things had happened since that last encounter in the surgical suite at HUP three years prior. Dr. J. would still be deemed to be on his last bit of gray matter, the arthroscope was now one-half the size, and there was something called fiberoptics which was hitting the surgical scene for the first time. Fiberoptics was a new light source where glass rods were used to pass the light to the tip of the instrument. This light source was so much better than the tungsten light source from my first arthroscopic encounter.

The inflow tubing was better, the drapes were better, the lighting was better, the arthroscope smaller, and our knowledge much greater. So, with this combination of better, Dr. J. and I did about six to eight of these arthroscopic examinations per day for patients who were known to have some degree of internal derangement of the knee. This procedure was starting to replace the x-ray test and the arthrogram with real time pictures of the condition inside this knee.

There were no surgical procedures associated with this diagnostic procedure at this time. The referring doctor got a report and, yes, a picture of the lesion. The norm for most knee surgeries at that time was for the primary surgeon to do his standard anterior cruciate repair or meniscectomy with the traditional Smillie meniscus knife. The ten-year literature at about that time was showing that people did very well for several years after the meniscectomy but at year five and beyond, the degree of arthritis would increase and would create increased disability.

This information about the long-term effects of taking the whole meniscus was now out, so the question became, "How do we remove less meniscus to lessen the negative effects of a meniscectomy? The answer was right in front of us every time we looked into a knee. These observations raised the next question, "How can we take out just the torn part of the meniscus and leave the rest alone?"

About this time, I suggested to Dr. J. that other specialties took out things in small places, like ENT. I visited the ENT department and borrowed some small 2-3 mm biters, also called cutters. We played with different types of biters and grabbers. We found a company that would make us tools for this purpose. I invested in a set of these tools and would have them for many years to come. They went everywhere with me. I would have them sterilized when I moved to new hospitals. This made me a change agent.

More rotations at more hospitals continued. Another one of my papers from my first-year research was published. One of the requirements in third year was that you had to do a project that needed to be completed by your senior year. I was now at that new Children's Hospital at the University of Pennsylvania, called Children's Hospital of Philadelphia (CHOP). This was the hospital that was just opening when I started my internship four years prior. Now as an orthopaedic resident at this hospital, I would pick my senior project. I was seeing a large number of kids with bowing of the legs. I did a good bit of research and found a number of children whose gait was being affected by this deformity. I started looking at who got better and who got worse with this deformity. The disease was called Blount's disease or tibia vara.

....If you can bear to hear the truth you've spoken

Twisted by knaves to make a trap for fools....

IF – by R. Kipling

The Chairman of the Pediatric Orthopedic division at CHOP gave the okay for this project. I continued to study the x-rays and started measuring different angles at different stages of the disease process. I performed a number of surgical procedures called percutaneous osteoclasts of the tibia to correct the bowing in those children with severe lower leg bowing. I had great success. I had something good going.

I discovered that I had two lines that I could get from each x-ray. One of these lines was called the epiphyseal line and the other line was a metaphyseal line. I followed the angle that these two lines made when they intersected. I called this the E-M Angle. This was an angle that had never been described. I determined that when the angle reached greater than twenty degrees, surgery was usually necessary to reverse the stress on the growth plate. Otherwise, an E-M Angle of less than twenty degrees, bracing would help; and, angles greater than twenty degrees, the damage to the growth plate would be progressive and bracing would not help. So, I had a developed a diagnostic and prognostic tool wrapped into one new E-M Angle which is still being used at the time of this writing.

My results were written up. I submitted my original research to the Commonwealth's, Pennsylvania Orthopedic Society (POS), who sponsors a yearly resident award contest. I was very pleased when I was notified that I was the winner of that year's award, and that I would be presenting my paper at the Annual POS convention in Bermuda–all expenses paid. This was the first order effect in winning this contest, but I had another paper to get published. The second order effect was jealousy in that my fellow residents believed that I had named the angle after myself, the E-M Angle of Blount's disease. If any one of them had elected to read my paper, they would have been able to determine E-M denoted the angle of the epiphyseal line and metaphyseal lines formed, which was the anatomical line formed by the growth plate and the angle marked the deformity of this abnormal relationship when found in this disease anatomy.

I dismissed these things as the "green-eyed monsters" at work. I did not have the time to get caught up in it. I went on into my last senior orthopedic year and I was back at Pennsylvania Hospital as the Chief Resident on the largest total hip-and-spine surgical service in all of Philadelphia—now two and one half years from that night when I left this hospital and never got home. I now had several junior residents that I oversaw who helped me run this very busy surgical service. These were the days that we did five to seven surgeries per day, twenty-five to thirty-five surgeries per week, 100-130 surgeries per month. In six months, you could see how many cases you had done or been a part of in that short course of time.

When I finished my Chief Residency, the Chairman said that I had been one of his best ever Chief Residents. I told him how glad I was that he came out that near fatal night in August and signed me out Against Medical Advice (AMA), four years earlier when I crashed. He had gotten me to the HUP where I got the best possible care and made a full recovery from that near fatal accident.

A summation of the last four years included: I now had one fellowship in orthopedic research done in my first year which had reaped several papers in peer review journals. I had won the Commonwealth of Pennsylvania's Orthopedic Resident Award and had another publication pending. I had completed the U of P orthopaedic residency in three years with a minor interruption of four months. I was now going to apply for my second fellowship because the University Hospital was recruiting one of the top sports medicine doctors to start a Sports Medicine Program at HUP. I applied to be the first sports medicine fellow at the HUP and I got it.

Dr. T. was the new doctor that HUP had lured away from another local sports medicine program. We hit it off quickly and were in full stride in quick order. I started another special project, this time with the department of anesthesia. I was using a regional block to do my shoulder surgery in order to use less postoperative pain medication. This simple reduction in postoperative pain medication could get the patient out of the hospital in a shorter period of time which was the evolving trend. I collected data on fifty of our next shoulder surgeries and did the study against fifty patients who had general anesthesia. I submitted the paper to the American College of Sports Medicine, and had it accepted. I would have to go to Big Sky, Montana, for the next Annual Meeting. Now, because I was the sports fellow, I had oversight with Dr. T. over all the sports teams.

I had always worked very hard and had been very lucky in my basketball sojourn, having gone to the NCAA tournament two times in my playing days. I was now about to make my third trip. This time, it would be as a team doctor for the University of Pennsylvania basketball team. The best part about this trip to the NCAA tournament was that we did not get knocked out in the first round. We did not get knocked out in the second round. As a matter of fact, we won the Eastern Regionals against the regional powerhouse on their home court and made it to the Final Four. Yes, we made it all the way to the Final Four!

We were bound for Salt Lake City, Utah, for the Final Four. We had a tough draw in the first game against the team from Michigan State. Although not the school I had turned down, University of

Michigan, when I switched at the last minute and went to St Joseph's College, but still a school in Michigan. It was that other Michigan school, Michigan State, and they had some guy who called himself, Magic, "Magic Johnson". Well, whatever his name was, and I am just kidding, because the University of Pennsylvania basketball, too, was way proud of a great season. We were going to have mid-court floor seating for one of the best finals in NCAA history and I was there.

Well, the outcome is now past history. The two basketball players from those two opposing teams, which came out of that Final Four, would have about eight NBA titles between them. Oh, yes, about the other team—Indiana State University. They were the favorite because they were undefeated at 31-0. They had somebody they called the "Bird Man" and his name was Larry Bird. I was sorry to see the trip end.

Chapter Thirteen

My fellowship in sports medicine was coming to an end and I was going to be forced to go out into the world and get a job. Philadelphia had been good to and for me. I was going to stay. I had a house here in the city and I would start my practice in short order.

I was to cut a deal with another doctor, a doctor of dentistry, who had become disabled secondary to a boating accident. He had an office in Center City Philadelphia which he was willing to rent to me since he had not used it in several years. However, he did not want his dental chairs removed from the exam rooms in case he came back into practice.

This occasion called for out-of-the-box thinking. That is, keep the dental chairs in place and make a sports medicine/orthopedic practice area. That was easy. Build my examination tables over the dental chairs after putting them in a reclined position and cover them. I did just that. I built three examination tables, six feet by thirty-six inches. I could elevate and lower the dental chair by foot pedal where I could reach it with my foot and I had examination tables that were motorized. I was ready to go. I had custom made examination tables that fit the doctor's 6 feet 6 inches in stature.

.....If you make one heap of all your winnings

And risk it on one turn of pitch-and-toss....

IF – by R. Kipling

All I needed now was $45,000 and a little extra, to open my doors. I needed $40,000 for malpractice insurance. I was about ready to sell my little house in Germantown because I wanted a Center City practice near the hospital where I had done some of my training. I was applying for admitting privileges to this hospital. I had not yet sold my house so I had to go to the bank for any new money. Very proud of my doctoral and post-doctoral education from the University of Pennsylvania, I went to the bank. They said no to my request for $45,000 to open my practice. What went wrong?

What when wrong was that I did not have a pro forma. A what? A pro forma? They told me I could get one done by my accountant, but I didn't have an accountant. So I went and got an accountant. I asked this accounting firm for someone who could help me with my pro forma. I was told that they could do a pro forma for me. Don Redcross was one of the senior partners of Levy & Redcross, an accounting firm in Philadelphia, and we met. He smiled at me with a sheepish grin and said he could do this pro forma for me.

I met with Mr. Redcross for several hours and answered a bunch of questions like: What would be the initial fee for an office visit? How long was my training for? How many surgeries did I think I would do a day, a month, and a year? I didn't know the first answer because I had no idea how I was going to see the first patient if I did not have malpractice insurance–and now I was going to get some bill for a pro forma.

Well, in forty-eight hours I met with Mr. Redcross again in my new office because I was in my paint clothes and I was painting the office for an unknown pending opening day. I got another one of those sheepish smiles from Mr. Redcross on his arrival. I did not

The Flow of Life

know where this pro forma thing was going. I put up my paint brush on the edge of the paint bucket and Mr. Redcross and I sat in my new partly-painted office.

Mr. Redcross pulled a document out of his briefcase and gave me a copy. He said that this was the pro forma that I had requested and I should submit to the bank for my loan. I opened the first page and the bottom of the page had a bunch of zeros. I asked him to go over this pro forma and he did. When he finished, my head was spinning and it was not from the paint fumes. This little pro forma said that I was going to make a lot of money. I asked, "How did you come up with these numbers?" He explained that he listened to me two days earlier used his accounting references to come up with the numbers.

This time when I went to the bank with my pro forma I thought the loan officer wanted to kiss me. This time this bank said yes to my $45,000 request. I was in business. Don Redcross would sit on my board and would be my corporate accountant for the next twenty years. I used a Professional Corporation (PC) as my business model, running my practice in a protective fashion into the malpractice world.

I was now off to find a partner so as not to be on call all the time, someone to work with, bounce things off and share the expenses of a practice. I found a guy who was getting ready to retire from the Navy, who was a Commander at the time we met. We met and talked, and agreed to practice together. Things got started but things did not work. The program did not work, because I think that, let's call him Dr. X., had no more "fire in the belly". Dr. X. would not come to his office hours on time and would make the patients wait for hours. He yelled at our receptionist and did not want to pay our bills on time. I had made a mistake.

I had to correct this mistake that I had made. I could not get him to leave so I left. I left my automatic exam tables. I now lived in town next door to this office. I had sold my house in Germantown. You might remember I had paid just over $13,000 dollars for it, but I sold it for $43,500. I went to give my aunt all her money back which she had lent me for the down payment, but she would not take it. So I was now looking for a building where I can both have an office and live.

I had a new patient that I acquired from the hospital when I was about to finish up my training at HUP. She followed me to my new office and now became my guardian angel. She always wanted to know how I ticked. The lady would not tell her age, but she was believed to be about seventy years old. She lived alone in Haddonfield, New Jersey. Her husband had been a lawyer but had been dead for a number of years. She was Mrs. F. She would show up at my office two to three times a week, saying she was just in town and she was stopping by to make sure I was doing okay.

She would always say, "You think you are a big shot." I would disagree with her. Then she would say, "But you are not, but I can help you." She was a big help when my partner would not perform. I needed to find a place. There was an old burned-out building across the street from my present office and next door to the apartment that my wife and I lived in. One day, when things were not going well at the present location, Mrs. F. said, "Why don't you buy the building across the street?" I told her I loved the location, but the building was a piece of junk. She then said that location, location, and location were the three most important things about that building.

The Flow of Life

So I was renting my apartment from a realtor whose office was on the first floor of this apartment building. I talked with him, Mr. BR. We took a walk through the building a week later and noted that most of the damage to the building was in the second floor front. The building had been sitting for about five years, but it had a lot of elegance and interesting architectural elements and needed a lot of work. I talked to Mrs. F. about it. She said that she had a bond that would give me the money to fix it up and would give me a mortgage. She even said that she would co-sign for the construction loan until the mortgage on the property was granted.

The big, then white, building had been a funeral home. The building was about 7,200 square feet. It was four stories high and was twenty-two feet wide and almost 100 feet long or deep. There was about two feet of water in the basement the first time I looked at the building. I could see the value and the vision of having such a building. I could make apartments in two of the floors, have my office on the first floor and we could live on the fourth floor. All I needed was a bucket of money. I had $40,000 from our closing and a pro forma that could be updated, complete with a co-signer if I needed one. I would get a construction loan for $100,000, I would buy the property for $100,000, and we could start the project. The project moved along and took about five months. I moved out of the joint office from across the street to my new office and our new apartment home. There were also two apartments in the building—one apartment on the second floor front and one two-story apartment on the second and third floor rear. Our apartment home was on the third and fourth floors in the front. The two apartments would be rented with tenants staying for the next eight to ten years.

Chapter Fourteen

During this time business was booming. I had also hired a Physician's Assistant (PA) because I was done with finding an orthopedic partner. My first attempt had been a disaster. I would not be ready to repeat it for some time. With a PA in my office, I would have someone that could extend my practice, help in surgery, and make rounds when I could not. The PA I found, was not a new find. He was an underclassman who came to St Joseph's College in my junior year. He was a good solid person. I interviewed him along with several other PA applicants. I picked my college alumnus. We were going to be a team for several years to come.

Rich, my PA, was already in the National Guard when he joined with me. We talked about how he got in and the benefits. He asked that I consider joining. I told him that I was "OK" and too busy. I was the president of the local medical society of minority physicians which was a chapter of the National Medical Association (NMA). This affiliation with the NMA went all the way back to my first year in medical school to the SNMA. I was recruiting doctors to increase the number in this local chapter. One of those physicians was a pediatrician that I knew. I asked if I could interest him in becoming more active with the local NMA chapter.

Dr. C. and I met to talk about his participation. He offered me to look at the National Guard where he was a Full Bird Colonel. He made several good points: You would be serving your country, you would get great leadership training, you would have a great routine, and it would keep you fresh. The last point he made was that if you did twenty years, you would have a great plan B for another income and healthcare for life. This was a case where the first shall be last and the last shall be first.

I talked it over with my wife and with my PA, who was already in this local unit under the command of Dr. C. After an okay from my wife, I asked Rich about his unit and asked if he would be my point man on drill weekend. Rich was overjoyed to do so, so I went from the "frying pan into the fire". I was given credit for all of my college time in Grade—undergraduate, medical school, internship, residency, and my two fellowships. I was given thirteen years of credit for pay, and, in grade, the rank of Captain. This would require one weekend per month and two weeks in the summer.

Dad had been in WWII and from when he passed several years earlier, I got his uniform that always hung in his closet, at the very end, on the left. So now his uniform hung in my closet, on the far left, with my new Dress Blues that I was required to get when I was commissioned. My Captain bars were on my uniform and all of his 1st Sgt. Stripes were on his. I learned very quickly that if I did my educational training in the Army, I could be promoted. If you did not do your training, you stayed the same rank. Going to school was already a major part of my life and makeup. If I was not studying something, I was not happy. Dad called education the great equalizer. In the Army, it was also true and I was going to prove it.

….Or being hated, don't give way to hating,

And yet don't look too good, nor talk too wise….

IF – by R. Kipling

I made the most of my drill weekends because I had never been one to waste time and sit and do nothing. My aggressive nature, Type A, bothered some people in the Army because they were just lazy and wanted to do the least of anything. One of these "green-eyed monsters" was holding my Army Personnel 201 file in the bottom of his desk drawer because such a move would freeze me in place. I knew I should have been up for promotion so I contacted Dr./Col. C. With a little reconciliation, my Army Personnel 201 file was found. The Army National Guard Bureau TAG had to promote me on the spot because I had gone way past my promotion day. I would have to be promoted or I would have to leave the Army. I was promoted to Major.

Understanding the political nature of the Army National Guard, I applied for a transfer to the United States Army Reserve. I was accepted and was now a Major. I moved to a new hospital unit. I continued with my schooling. I would soon be looking at another promotion in a couple of years. I stayed the course with my weekend duty calls and the two-week summer exercises. This was just the start of a twenty plus year sojourn with the United States Army Reserve.

I would practice my sports medicine and othopaedics and live at this Pine Street location for about the next five years. The practice grew by leaps and bounds.

I had waited six years into marriage to have children because the medical training was too demanding to do both. My wife had agreed at the time. Now, with me in practice with a home, I believed it was a good time to start a family. My wife disagreed and did not want to have my children. She did not like the life of a doctor's wife. My wife wanted out, a divorce, so I gave her something better. I went to the Catholic Church and had our marriage annulled. She then left the city with a new partner. I have neither seen nor spoken with her since she left our apartment home. Good luck and God's speed.

I was very involved in the state, the city, and my university medical societies. My old college was now a university. I became the president of the medical society for my old university. I would get a chance to honor two of my mentors by nominating them for our top honor from the Medical Society of Saint Joseph's University. The first person was someone who was world renowned, Dr. C Everett Koop, Surgeon General of the United States of America. Dr. Koop had separated the first set of Siamese twins at the Children's Hospital of Philadelphia (CHOP). He also headed the pediatric surgical residency position for CHOP during what was my senior year in medical school. I was shocked when this Professor of Pediatric Surgery stopped me in the hallway of CHOP one afternoon and asked if I would consider applying for his surgical program. I did not even know he knew who I was. Dr. Koop posed that, yes, he knew who I was and that he did not normally stop people in the hallway and offer them a position in his residency program. I begged his pardon and told him of my love for orthopaedics and my future hopes and plans.

The second person was my orthopaedic mentor, Dr. Jim E. Nixon. James E. Nixon, MD, Chairman of the Department of Orthopedic Surgery, at The Graduate Hospital, was the smartest man I ever knew. He was an old fashioned doctor who could fly off the handle at any second of any day. But he always had a measured purpose for whatever his did. He taught me that whatever you do, become the expert. This was very important to me because I had a testing problem. My reading and testing problems were discovered to be something called dyslexia. I took his advice and moved ahead throughout arthroscopic surgery as the go-to person in orthopedic/arthroscopic surgery. I would be a part of a sports radio program on sports injuries. I would even get a chance to travel with five Olympic teams from around the world. I would be an Olympic doctor for about ten years. I would be selected to be doctor-in-residence for the 1988 Olympic Team in Colorado Springs, Colorado.

Chapter Fifteen

I worked harder and longer days and had paid off the construction loan. I now had a mortgage on the building, but I did not have anyone to come home to. I dated for about a year without any number one rising to the top. I was on five boards around town and these social functions kept me busy. I was now past thirty-five years of age, and I wouldn't be getting any younger. I was the co-chair of the Philadelphia Easter Seal annual fundraiser, and I invited my broker and his wife from NYC to this event. They came along with another couple from New York. The other couples, a lawyer and his girlfriend, were also both from NYC. The dinner ended early and I invited my New York broker and their friends back to my apartment home. A good evening was had by all. We exchanged cards with the new couple and the evening ended.

Three months later, I received a message in my post-surgical telephone pile that one of the visiting couples had called. I remember the very tall Latino lady, Norma, from that night. After I did the urgent messages, I settled back into my office chair and returned her call. I had to retrieve the card from the lawyer boyfriend so I could remember his name. I remembered her. I dialed the number and she answered. I said that it was nice to hear from her after all this time. I asked how her lawyer friend was and I called him by name with his card laid out in front of me on my desk. She broke the news to me that they had broken up and she was moving on. I asked when she would be coming to the city again. She said that she was taking a road trip and would be coming through Philly in about one week. I asked if she would stop and maybe we could have dinner.

Well, I cleared the deck for her arrival and canceled all the plans that were already on the books. She came and we hit it off really well. She was one of two children. Her father was a doctor and her mother was an educator. She loved to travel and worked for Pan Am Airlines. She had a degree in psychology from Cornell University.

We shared all our past failures and talked about all of our future hopes. Children and travel were just two things that closed the deal. Six weeks later I asked Norma to marry me. Ten weeks later we were married. We had receptions in Philly and NYC because it was a quick turnaround. About one year later, a morning pregnancy test verified that our first child was on its way.

Life around trips to NYC, Brazil, and Europe was the order of the day for the next couple of years. I was working with the US Olympic team and was asked to go to Brazil with the US Roller Hockey team. Our first son, Justino Ignacio, was eighteen months old and the team's mascot for that trip. Our second son, Marcos Alejandro, was to arrive three months after that trip and life went on now with my wife and two sons.

I would go to the First Arthroscopic Meeting in Salt Lake, Utah. A Canadian named, Dr. D. Jackson, who had done a lot of arthroscopic work, was presenting at this meeting and I wanted to learn from him. The course was great and I came home now able to do a lot of my surgery under local anesthesia. In this way, the patient did not have to stay in the hospital overnight. The whole concept of day surgery was taking a foothold. One of my mentors told me on my return from my out-west trip that not everybody was going to do this. However, within the next three years, it became a mandate to do knee surgery as an outpatient only. I was a vision mover for my time in this space.

The marketplace was changing with new equipment and everything was now in the forefront. Arthroscopic surgery was done with water as the expansion medium inside the knee. There was a major drug company that wanted to introduce a $CO2$ laser for arthroscopic surgery. I tried it. I liked it and did a number of arthroscopic laser surgeries in Philadelphia. I flew off and got more training at the Grant Laser Center in Ohio. I was keeping pace and I was setting pace. I was then asked to travel around the country to teach other doctors how to use this $CO2$ laser. In about eighteen months, the larger company sold its Laser Division to a small company and the interest faded. Doctors who had started doing arthroscopic surgery with water flow were not likely to change.

For me, I used this period to drive business my way. I invested in a road-side billboard on I-95 into Philadelphia. I paid for the billboard for about eight months and then got about sixteen more months out of the billboard by the time the billboard was being changed at the end of a contract for some other vendor. "For Laser Arthroscopic Surgery, call 238-Bone." This 238-Bone was our phone number for our practice from the time we started in the new building on Pine Street until I closed my office in Philadelphia twenty-two years later on Vine Street.

The family had grown. We were going to run a bilingual household because I hated to be behind either eight ball or the curve. With a Latino wife, I did not know who her family and friends were talking about at birthday and holiday gatherings. I wanted to make sure it was not about me. I knew I had to learn Spanish. So I did! We got a friend of a friend to find someone to help with the children to learn Spanish and for me to learn Spanish. I had to be the first one to learn Spanish. The army was another reason to learn Spanish because I was getting a new promotion and a special operations unit with civil affairs had an opening. I only spoke Spanish to the boys, as bad as it was. We took vacations to Puerto Rico and Spain. I had every object in the house labeled so I could learn the vocabulary. It worked!

The office space was becoming tight. My physical therapists were working in the very back of the office. I was sharing rooms with them. I had expanded into the basement which we called the lower level. The waiting room was getting too small. The family was getting larger and we wanted to separate the home from the office. Most people now knew that we lived over the office.

There was a pretty house on Tryon Street one-half block from South Street. The house on Tryon Street was special with a courtyard and the price was right. We would rent our apartment home with the other two apartments and let the building carry itself. There was a 40,000 sq. ft. building that a group, Mrs. F., RB, and two other investors had an interest in. We put together a limited partnership, put in our money and pledged to use a percentage of the space in the building. I knew what I wanted to do. My mentor, Dr. R., had his institute, and I wanted mine. I am a dreamer!

If you can dream—and not make dreams your master;

IF – by R. Kipling

I put in my money to buy the building. I took my part of this 40,000 sq. ft. property and called it The Institute for Musculoskeletal Disorders and Sports Medicine. I had a neurologist who was coming out of training and lured him because he wanted a private practice without the private practice risk of being out in the market place solo. I was also able to have a doctor of internal medicine. A physical therapy group also moved into the building and their practice took off. I still had their loyalty to take care of my patients.

I opened the South Street practice and Institute with a party to end all parties. The Mayor of Philadelphia came. State Representatives and Senators, who didn't need an agenda to make their presence known if they were up for election, came. In addition, the President of St Joseph's University was also there. Touchingly, he had also on that day presented me with my framed basketball jersey, number 34 from St. Joseph's University. I had combined this opening with an art show which included all of the Black Artists of Philadelphia among others. We had about 3,000 people for this opening and ribbon cutting. South Street was blocked off for this event. Life was good.

You can only hope that people do what they say they are going to do. Out of five partners in the South Street building deal, I was the only one who did what I said I was going to do. Dad always said, "Your word is your bond"! I moved my office into the building. I renovated my space started paying our corporation rent for my space. My physical therapy group, as part of my team had their space done and The Sports Medicine Institute was up and operational. We lived on Tryon Street and practiced on South Street. The two locations were 300 yards from each other.

Living and working close had one limitation only. My then four-year-old son, Justin, decided to leave the house for that 300 yard journey one late afternoon. He came looking for me when the nanny's back was turned. She was tending to his two-year-old brother, Marcus. My wife arrived home shortly thereafter and asked where the oldest was. In short order, the alarm went out. I got a panic phone call while out doing some shopping. With the pedal to the metal, I started my trip to the house. A canvas of the area quickly determined that he may not have been looking for me because he ended up in the corner Pizza Shop fifty yards beyond the office's front door. The pizza storeowner got the police to come and get him. A call to the local police station and one son retrieved resulted in my heartbeats returning to normal.

My main hospital was two blocks away from the office and my plans for family, home and practice were working. Life went on and our first son would soon start nursery school nearby. We had a second nanny from Columbia who lived with us and helped with the kids. The house was starting to get small and my wife wanted to move to a bigger house. However, this would put us out of the city. A commute into and out of Philly everyday was not my idea of a good time.

Weighing all the options, I suggested that we sell the Tryon house and move back into Pine Street. I agreed that we would take Pine Street, give notice to our tenants, and we could take the whole Pine Street building and make it our home. We could take the old physical therapy location in the back of the property and convert to a garage. Our first floor office space would become our formal living room and dining room. The old examination rooms would be made into a billiards and game room. The second floor rear would be my home office and library.

The Flow of Life

The second floor front, which was a one bedroom apartment, would now be our master bedroom suite with sauna and Pullman kitchen. The third floor, a two-story apartment would become the kitchen and den with bedrooms upstairs. All of the four fireplaces were opened and lined for full operation. This was now a dream house. We were asked to put our home as part of the yearly Rittenhouse Square Historic Homes Tour. We did so for several years until it became more difficult as the children got older.

Chapter Sixteen

My military reserve career continued along with all the other components of my life. Col C. had been promoted to Brigadier General in the National Guard and I was now a Lieutenant Colonel (LTC) in the United States Army Reserve. I had moved several times to several different units to promote my changes of advancement. I continued my military training and used my benefits from the Army to get a number of continuing medical education (CME) credits that I need every two years for my medical licensure for several states that I was licensed in.

….And so hold on when there is nothing in you

Except the Will which says to them: "Hold on"….

IF – by Rudyard Kipling

A position in a Special Operation PYSO unit opened in my area and I jumped at it because I wanted to go to Jump School. The position would be the Public Health Officer for the 359th Civil Affairs Unit. I applied for the job. I had several people in my interview try to talk me out of it. One person explained that Special Operations did not live by the normal standards of the US Army but had special requirements for physical fitness testing, special language and swimming proficiently. There was also a rough 10 kilometer rucksack march which was required on a timed course. I said bring it on and vowed to always finish ahead of the people that questioned my ability to get it done. On my first rucksack march, with a 65 pound load, which was required, I finished second in the Unit. My interviewer who questioned my ability was not number one.

This assignment and position would take me to the Pentagon for a pre-invasion meeting and my first deployment to Haiti in Operation Joint Task Force (JTF 180).

On the orthopaedic front, I was still writing papers and submitted one to the International Medicina de Rehabilitation on rehabilitation after laser surgery. My paper was accepted. My wife and I went to Spain so I could present the paper. We were going to make it a business and pleasure trip. We planned a one week stay. We landed in Madrid where the conference was. I gave my paper the next day. It was well received. After the presentation, we had five more days to see Spain. I rented a car and started driving. We drove south. We had no hotel and no fixed plans. We stopped at different points of interest. Two days later, we stopped for lunch at a beachfront café on the Costa del Sol.

When I say beachfront, I mean beachfront. We had to take off our shoes because the waves were coming up to and under the table. Our major problem now was that we had no beach towels in our luggage. A solution quickly arrived. A pretty young lady approached us from the beach and asked if we would like to take a tour of a new timeshare, just one hundred meters down the road. We both thanked her but said no thank you. However, her final words were, "We have a coupon for dinner for two and a free beach towel." There were our beach towels. So we both said okay to dinner and the beach towels.

After lunch, we went on a tour of this new resort complex. It was beautiful and it overlooked the Mediterranean Sea. It had two bedrooms, three bathrooms, and a deck/terrace to die for. I knew nothing about this concept that was called a timeshare. I listened and we were put up for the night after we received dinner. After a careful review of the deal, I liked what I saw and bought four weeks of our timeshare on the Costa del Sol.

The whole family would return the next year, with Justin five years old and Marcus just turning four years old. With my wife's request for more family time, I closed the practice for one month of vacation for the next twelve years. My office staff was able to work on receivables and catch up on all the things that had not been done those other eleven months. The process worked very well. I had to schedule my two weeks with the Army Reserve so that it did not conflict with the family vacation.

The yearly trips to Spain worked very well when I went to the 1992 Olympics as part of their medical team. We spent the first two weeks of that summer vacation in Barcelona, Spain, at the Olympics and went to our place in Marbella on the Costa del Sol for the last two weeks of August. The late night discussion between my wife and me was talk of how the medical industry was changing and the fact that I would have to make some changes in order to stay in the game and become a mover of this end-game.

Just prior to the 1988 Olympics, I was the Doctor-in-Residence at the United States Olympic Team training facilities in Colorado Springs, Colorado. I was invited by a fellow Olympic team doctor whom I knew and had trained with during my traveling Sports Medicine Fellowship in Los Angeles, CA during my sports medicine fellowship year at Penn and HUP. Dr. H. knew I was in Colorado Springs at the training center and asked if I would cover the US

Olympic Basketball team when they played an exhibition game in Denver, Colorado. I said I would do so with pleasure. Dr. H. was a fellow Olympic team doctor whom I knew and had trained with during my traveling Sports Medicine Fellowship in Los Angeles, CA during my sports medicine fellowship year at Penn and HUP.

That short trip to Denver had long ties back to Washington, DC. Two of the coaches for the US Olympic team were Washington, DC guys that I knew very well. JT and GR were basketball players and coaches who were a few years older. They had set the pace for us to follow.

I was in the Army now for almost ten years and had done all of my schooling. I was sent to Virginia Beach and Norfolk, Virginia for Command and General Staff School. I had completed it and got promoted to Light Colonel. I applied for an open position with a Civil Affairs Unit in Norristown, Pennsylvania, which is a short drive from Philadelphia.

Chapter Seventeen

Civil Affairs was part of the Psychological School of Operations (PSYO), a division of Special Operations (SO) in the John F. Kennedy School at Ft. Bragg in North Carolina. I had an interview with the Commander of a detachment of the 359th Civil Affairs Unit, who tried to talk me down from taking the position, telling me how tough it was being in Special Operations. He told me that Special Operations minimums exceeded the regular army's maximums. This didn't faze me and I told him so.

I took the position as the Public Health Officer for the 359th Civil Affairs Unit and couldn't wait for our first PT test and forced march so I could smoke him. I smoked him on that first PT run and rucksack 10 km march. I never ever heard another word from him on this issue of tough.

The Army and Spain vacations cycled around a couple more times. None of the other partners in the South Street deal had moved into the building. The Army was looking at a Haiti problem. During that summer vacation in Spain, I had to fly back to the USA and go to the Pentagon because some type of military action was going to take place. I had to meet with the Director Pan American Health Organization (PAHO), because they were feeding over 700,000 people in Haiti and did not want this service to be interrupted if possible.

I was the Public Health Officer for the 359th Civil Affairs Unit which was attached to the 82nd Airborne. So where the 82nd went, we went as their CA package.

The Flow of Life

Civil Affairs is one of the first noncombat packages that come into a country with or without combat. We are first, because Civil Affairs is the major part of the operational exit strategy. Civil Affairs is how to put the lights back on, help to get water flowing again and get the public health components working, from hospitals, to schools, to prisons. I got back to Spain with the family and we continued our Costa del Sol refueling vacation.

It was not long after we had returned from Spain when I got the phone call for me to go to report for Active Duty. Haiti, I think! I was in my Orthopaedic/Sports Medicine office when a call came from my local Reserve unit. The order had come down. I was advised to pick up my weapon from the unit. My order would be faxed to me in short order.

I had a practice that I had to shut down in four hours and get on a flight to upstate New York. I received my orders and I was off to Philadelphia International Airport after a short stop to my Center City home to grab my already packed rucksack. A quick kiss to the boys and my wife with "I will call you with some details as soon as I know some details" and off I was.

Philadelphia to Syracuse, New York, was the flight I was catching. It's now 6:30 pm and I have an army detail picking me up in Syracuse so I can in-process at Fort Drum, New York, about a one and one-half hour trip from the airport. My call to Active Duty orders are for ten days with no more information than to report to Fort Drum, New York, by 2300 hr. on that day. At 0600 hour the same morning, I was making rounds and discharging patients from the hospital. Now 1700 hours later, I am in my Battle Dress Uniform (BDU) being in-processed by the 10th Mountain Division personnel for Operation JTF 180.

The next several days brought a number of meetings and a lot of shots and pills for the local deployment protocol. Still no word of when, but we all knew the where. About day four, new orders were issued for 180 days of Active Duty in Operation Uphold Democracy. The 359th Civil Affairs unit would be attached to the 82nd Airborne. We were to be on ground in the area of operation (AO) on D+1 in support of the mission. While on the tarmac for over twelve hours, the mission got changed twice. The JTF 180 went to JTF 185, to JTF 190. These numbers relate to the about of force that, will or was planned to be used for introduction into a said AO. Well, the operation went from a 3000 Airborne Combat Jump order to an invitation for entry from the host nation. This pushed our entry date up to "D-day".

C-130s, the aircraft for troop transport took us into Haiti on "D-day". With a late arrival after dark in Haiti's International Airport, one of the hangers at the airport became home for the next twelve hours. You had to find a place to sleep. All of the soldiers were responsible for themselves with their rucksacks. I was so glad that I had my combat hammock and was able to keep off the ground where rodents had their run, no thank you.

The 359th CA lead unit had a forty-two personnel pack in this advance party in which I was included. We moved out the next day to an industrial warehouse that was the command center for this operation. We got our Civil Affairs headquarters' set-up and I was off to work in my area of concentration, Public Health.

I had been studying the state of the nation from a health standpoint for some time and had gone to the Pentagon for meetings with the Pan American Health Organization (PAHO) prior to our planned invasion, now an invitation via a deal that would not be disclosed for some time. Our invasion, thank God, was downgraded to a humanitarian invitation into this island country. Haiti had been brutalized and raped by a military coup which had forced the President of Haiti to abdicate to Washington DC for political amnesty. The then President of the United States of America and Commander in Chief, Bill Clinton, ordered the military action to uphold democracy for the small nation state. The citizens of Haiti were leaving Haiti by all means possible on anything that would flow into the open sea.

The United States Coast Guard that patrolled the waters off of the coast of the United States was rescuing hundreds of Haitians per day which included men, women and children who were in the water on anything that would or could float and many times did not. Many Haitians lost their lives in their attempt to escape the terror of this rogue military that were raping and killing at will.

My job for the next ninety-three days would be to try to restore some order to the health and welfare system for this island's population and country. I would make nightly and daily reports to the Commanding General for this operation. I would make inspections of hospitals, prisons and health clinics throughout the island. The conditions of these institutions were not good and long range planning was started. I would welcome the director of PAHO when he arrived to the island about one week after our arrival.

The director of PAHO and I had first met at a Pentagon planned meeting in Washington, DC about six weeks before the planned invasion. His bequest to me as the Public Health Officer of this task force, in our earlier meeting, was that the United States Army not feed the people of Haiti. He explained that there were more than 800 Non-Governmental Organization (NGOs) and Private

Voluntary Organizations (PVOs) feeding more than 850,000 Haitians daily. He did not want another food system started for feeding the people of Haiti which could and would go away after the democratic government was restored and the major numbers of the US military left. I was at the foot of the stairs as he descended the stairs onto the island. We exchanged hellos and I told him that I had kept our deal and was not planning to or have fed the people of Haiti.

Leaving the airport that day, I was stopped and interrogated by a two star General as to why I, a LTC was at the airport. This then LTC, explained the reason for my necessary visit and explained to him that I was reporting nightly to a three star General at Command Headquarters. The two-star general, General C. and I became buddies during our time on the Island. I would be invited to his G-2 section at the Pentagon multiple times up until General C retired.

I was also working with the United States Agency for International Development with (USAID). They wanted to put some money into their economy and gave me $5,000 to spend in the name of health. My question became what could I do with $5,000 to help the greatest number of people on this island. Perhaps it would be $5,000 of bottled water because of the high mortality rate secondary to diarrhea in infants and young children? No, there was no lasting effect after the water and the $5,000 was gone. Still working on where to spend this money, I got information, a situation report (sitrep), that the USS Comfort had arrived in the Port au Prince harbor. The USS Comfort had been ordered to move from Cuba to Port au Prince to assist. The Comfort had wash-kits that were being used for the Haitians that the Coast Guard was picking out of the sea and taking them in great numbers to Guantanamo Bay, Cuba, for repatriation back to Haiti.

The Flow of Life

Now, with the Island under US occupation to uphold democracy, the flood of Haitians leaving their island had stopped. The Comfort had several thousands of these kits which contained several different types of washing devices in each kit.

I requested and then had to go and receive these 3,000 care kits from the USS Comfort which I did. I took possession of these care kits and I knew right away how the $5,000 from USAID would be used to have the greatest impact on the greatest number of people. The $5,000 would buy 10,000 bars of soap and the care kits would be separated by their different container size within the care kit. A care container and a bar of soap would be given to the schools to teach hand washing to all grade age children. This would be a school program in hand washing and how to stop disease.

One other public health project which would affect hundreds of thousands of the island's children was my Cold-Point project. This project was to put thirty-two propane refrigerators in thirty-two different clinics throughout the island for the purpose of immunization from childhood diseases for the children. There had been a recent outbreak of measles after the dry ice evaporated in a measles inoculation program on the island. All the good health education and disease prevention was interrupted because the vaccines had no Cold Point. Now, with operation "Cold Point", storage of vaccines would not be a problem.

I traveled most days by helicopter to different parts of the island which was difficult if not impossible by land. During my tour of duty in Haiti, I had the unpleasant duty of going and getting a body of one of the doctors from, Doctors without Borders, who had died from a heart attack, while trying to make other people lives better.

In the meantime, my private practice back home was on "life support" because while I was away, there was no cash flow. All the back-billing had kept things afloat for a while, but the practice was now on "life support". I ask for release from the 180 days orders. My new orders were amended to ninety days and I was homebound several days later. However, just before I left for home, I received word that I have been selected for 0-6 Colonel. About that same time, the three-star commanding General for this task force was awarded his 4th Star. I wrote him and congratulated him in my letter and he did the same for me.

Chapter Eighteen

I returned home to my family, my practice and a job offer to become Senior Vice President of Medical Affairs for a failing inter-city healthcare system. The hospital system was set in the lower end of North Philadelphia. City Hall, the epicenter for Philadelphia, was within its view from Broad Street less than twenty blocks from William Penn on top of City Hall. However, with the hospital 52 million dollars in the red, things were not looking good.

I had interviewed for this position before I got called to active duty for Haiti. The hospital administration thought I was the man for the job and started writing letters to the US Army and the President of the United States, requesting my release from my call to duty as soon as possible because of the needs of the hospital community in North Philadelphia back here in the United States of America. I accepted the job on my return to Philadelphia, and took a few of my chief personnel with me to the hospital. I was able to keep my private practice of orthopaedics and sports medicine in full swing with a marked reduction in overhead. I was also able to deflect the growing cost of malpractice insurance, as well, my two largest salaries, and half of my salary was now absorbed by the hospital.

It was now time to put to use all that leadership training that I had been engaged in for over a decade via my military schooling. I was able to recruit a large group of great young doctors to our staff and replaced many of the old department heads, who were accustomed to doing things "their way" because this is "the way" we have always done it. New people with new thinking were able to help change the culture of the North Philadelphia Health System. All the ports of entry to the hospital that had been blocked by abandoned housing were leveled, rehabilitated or turned into local parks, making new ports-of-entry for the community-at-large. "Build it and they will come."

With the acute care hospital's days-to-receivables cut in half, an operating room that doubled in cases, length of stay on the decline and a white coat wearing medical staff, this acute care hospital was ready for our next survey by the Joint Commission on Accreditation of Healthcare Organizations (JCAHO). The last survey, just two years prior to my arrival, was a conditional pass with a score of 77 and a number of corrective actions needed for the hospital to remain Medicare certified and the doors open.

Armed with a new computerized medical staff operational suite of improvements and a new mission statement, "Quality Healthcare with Prevention, Education and Treatment" (Q-PET) which every member of the hospital staff knew, the hospital was on its way to an unconditional 96% JCAHO score. This was the work of a lot of people with a special thanks to my Assistant Vice-President of Medical Affairs, Ms. A, also my long-time left-arm person, Melinda M, whom I brought with me for this challenging task and works with me to this date.

With this joint effort, we were able to get this community hospital back on solid ground and at the time of this writing, twenty years later, this hospital is still serving the community. One of those two employees that I took with me in 1994, Carolyn S., is still there today and heads the operating room where she started on her arrival with me at the start of my SVP run.

Now I have three principal jobs, Senior Vice President of Medical Affairs for a hospital corporation, an orthopaedic surgical practice fifteen years in the making and responsibilities as a newly promoted Full Bird Colonel in the United States Army Reserve. I can, I will, I must!

Chapter Nineteen

My job now was to find a new job to fit my new promotion with the USAR to Colonel. There was a Combat Support Hospital (CSH) in New York which was without a commander. This was within striking distance with less than a two-hour drive from Philly. I requested an interview for this position. I got the interview and the job. I was questioned as to why I would want this unit, the 343rd CSH, because the Commanding General denoted, this unit was broken, with the readiness of this unit being at the lowest in the readiness structure. My answer was, "I only see one way, I can take this unit, and it's up."

Over the next three years, we took the civilian hospital and my Army hospital to new heights. Back in Philadelphia another JCAHO survey at one of the three hospitals in our corporate structure was due for its accreditation. With systems in place for over two years now, we were able to score a perfect score of 100% on our JCAHO survey. Our hospital was the only hospital in the Commonwealth of Pennsylvania that year to receive a perfect score of 100. I saluted the staff for a job well done.

The 343rd CSH back in New York had some special talents which we put to good use to raise our value proposition. I had a large number of bilingual Spanish speaking soldiers that put the 343rd CSH in a special class to do Medical Readiness Training Programs (MEDREDS) in our southern Area of Operations (AO) of Mexico, Central America and South America. MEDREDS were like the

The Flow of Life

public relation arm of the Army. A MEDRED would be developed with the host country to send in twenty-five to forty doctors, dentists and nurses for ten days to an area of their country which didn't have the resources which the 343rd CSH could bring to bear.

MEDREDS gave the 343rd a new sense of purpose and each soldier found a new sense of being and the unit sprung to life. As soon as one MEDRED was done, I would be looking for a new one for our "Combat Ready" unit, somewhere in the world. The 343rd CSH was a combat support hospital with a "Combat Ready" credo. I injected this credo into the unit on the first day of my arrival because I knew that we would need something to hang our hats on. With my introduction to the unit soldiers, I explained that we as a hospital may never see combat, but our principal job was to make every soldier that passed through our doors, no matter the reason, "Combat Ready" and to get him or her back into the fight to ensure victory for the USA. Soon, making injured soldiers "Combat Ready" became our mission, our credo and our battle cry. Every unit formation or meeting would find every soldier on their feet and pronouncing "Combat Ready" at the top of their lungs, as I entered the field or meeting room.

....Or being hated, don't give way to hating,

And yet don't look too good, nor talk too wise....

IF – by Rudyard Kipling

This unit cohesion and unification was by no means a single result of a new commander. But, as the new commander, I had the responsibility to create a team of leaders which could and would take this unit to the top. My first objective was to have my executive officer

(XO) in sync with the commander's intent. This meant every staff officer, including the XO, must know what I wanted and needed to achieve our mission on a day-to-day basis of being "Combat Ready". My present XO came up a little short on this note because he, too, had put in for this command as a medical service officer. This position would have taken him to the highest field rank of Colonel a 0-6 command which I now held. This was going to make our climb to the top tough if not impossible, if he stayed in this unit.

Shortly after my arrival to the unit I called my XO in and asked him to seek another position outside of the 343rd CSH. I explained that I needed someone that understands and could carry out my intent. I called LTC Morgan with whom I had worked ten years earlier and asked if he would become me XO for the 343rd CSH. He accepted. The commander's intent would be understood by this seasoned soldier. I cut a deal with my Command Sergeant Major, E-9, who had plans to retire prior to my arrival, to stay with me just six months and take command of the non-commissioned troops until I could find a replacement for him. He consented to give me those six months.

Running a reserve CSH unit that met one weekend a month and two weeks in the summer, a full-time staff Army Guard Reserve (AGR) staff in accordance with the Table of Organization and Equipment (TO&E) for a CSH was critical to our readiness for missions that could ignite at any hour of any day. The full-time AGR positions for personnel S1 and operations S3 were the two critical positions that had to be addressed. I was blessed to have two AGR Majors who had recently joined the unit as full-time AGR's. Majors R and S were my S1 and S3 and were very happy to read into the commander intent. My command staff was now formed with all the critical positions filled and we were working toward becoming "Combat Ready".

The Flow of Life

Meanwhile, back in the civilian world, the hospital and the orthopaedic practice were in full swing. I knew however, that I needed some more education in hospital finance and other administrative skills to function at the highest level in my senior position in this hospital corporation. Over the next year, I would take a number of courses to become a Certified Physician Executive (CPE) through the American College of Physician Executives.

On the home front, my two sons were coming of school age. We lived in Center City Philadelphia over the office at that time. There was one school that my wife liked but it required a forty-five minute bus ride every day to Germantown. I had been bused around for school but in the 1950s it was for another reason—segregation. Brown vs the Board of Education did not pass until 1954 and I was already in school. If you could call it a school! It was three rooms in a little building, which had two grades one through six in the three rooms. The bathroom was an outhouse and the building had no plumbing.

I believed that we needed to use our present and local school system if we were going to be an active part of the community. I won this round and Justin, our oldest son, started the local school where he could walk to school with the boys and girls whom we lived around. Marcus would join his brother two years later. Justin was ultimately tested and invited to be admitted to our local magnet school, the prestigious Julia Reynolds Masterman Laboratory and Demonstration School, in Philadelphia.

Justin would spend eight years at this magnet school, winning the Spanish language award several times during his tenure. On the playing field of sports, Justin had no interest in the hardwoods of the basketball court and found a liquid platform to become All-City in Swimming and Captain of the High School City Championship, also, for two years.

Back to my CSH, once a month, it was by no means a one weekend a month job. I talked with my full-time staff almost every day just to plan for the weekend drill arrival of up to 400 Combat Ready soldiers from every walk of life to have them morph into a CSH that had a mission of keeping our fighting units in the fight. Remember, the members of 343rd CSH are doing MEDREDS all over Central America and it was the most talked about unit in the 8th Medical Brigade. I was selected to attend the National Defense School and continued to learn new skills. Command tenure for a CSH is three years with a one-year extension that can be requested. My tenure with the 343rd CSH was coming to a close. I had to consider asking for an extension of one year or to find a new command. Having a second command would put me very high on the promotion list to move to become a General Officer. The other component, which helped to drive the General Officer train, was to be accepted to and complete the United States Army War College (USAWC). I applied to the USAWC in Carlisle, Pennsylvania.

My S1 about then brought to my attention that the 369th CSH in Puerto Rico (PR) was looking for a new commander. This unit was known to be mission capable but was listed as a Bad Boy Unit, and was, therefore, not at the top of anyone's list for MEDREDS or other deployments. I had been to PR many times because my wife's parents were both from PR and many family visits at Christmas and holidays were made to PR. I had been working on my Spanish since the kids were born so I was willing to learn some more Spanish.

However, what I knew from my first command was that my full-time AGR, S1 and S3 were the critical elements that I needed to make a reserve unit tick. So, I went to my S3, Major Smithson, first and told him about the possible new command in PR. I told him that I would consider taking this new command only if he would go with me. It took only two words, "Yes, Sir." "Yes, Sir, what," I said. "Do you understand what I am talking about, or Yes, Sir, I will go with you. Which one is it, the former or the latter, Major?" "The latter, Sir. I will go with you anywhere, Sir." This Major had been my soldier's soldier for this command and it took him just enough time to say "Yes, Sir" in his decision making process. We both then went to see the S1 who was from Puerto Rico (PR) and asked if he could return to PR as my S1. He gave a conditional yes because he had to talk with his wife.

In 1999, DeMatha High School honored me by accepting me into their Hall of Fame. I traveled back to the Washington DC area to accept this gracious and prestigious award. My picture now hangs on the wall of DeMatha High School, Hyattsville Maryland. The same year I graduated from the United States Army War College. There, my name is engraved on that wall as well. These two years were two of the most demanding because of all the coursework that I had to deliver weekly in addition to on-campus work in the summer. Special thanks go to several people that served to read these papers and put them into understandable English. Those people know who they are. Siempre, to them.

To leverage those two years of work at the Army War College, I enrolled into a Master's Program for International Relations at Salve Regina University in Newport Rhode Island. I saw the world becoming flat and wanted to be ready. I knew that the Army Way

College degree would soon be accredited into a Master's Degree in Strategy but couldn't take the risk of not getting the benefits of these two hard and trying years into a Master's degree. So I did both. Salve Regina, would accept, as many other colleges, all of the credits from the United States Army War College. So I parlayed my coursework from the USAWC into several more courses at Salve Regina and presto, two degrees. Yes, I was a degree junky because I had grown up with the belief that a degree was something no one could take away from you once you earned it.

....If you can talk with crowds and keep your virtue,

Or walk with kings – nor lose the common touch....

IF – by Rudyard Kipling

Chapter Twenty

Back in Philly town, I was having some very nice articles written about me in the local newspapers and Physician Executive magazine, among others.

….If neither foes nor loving friends can hurt you;

If all men count with you, but none too much….

IF – by Rudyard Kipling

I was interviewed by many people over the years and articles were written about me in newspapers and magazines. It made me feel good that I was perceived as making a difference.

18 NOVEMBER•DECEMBER 2001 THE PHYSICIAN EXECUTIVE

….Graffiti patrol! He points out the flora in a tiny park outside, a spot where Mitchell successfully lobbied Philadelphia City Hall to tear down two abandoned houses. On the surrounding streets, Mitchell led doctors and hospital staff in an annual cleanup that helped rid of the area of graffiti.

Mitchell—also a career Army reservist who was the chief public health officer when U.S. troops restored the democratic elected government of Haiti in 1994—added several touches of military-style discipline to a hospital that had gotten a little sloppy. He opens up a metal coat locker to a display a row of gleaming, laundered physician coats. Department chief names are embroidered in red; other doctors get their names in blue. "I think it's important to have a chain of command," says Mitchell, whose towering stature, salt-and-pepper hair and paisley green bow-tie lend him an air of authority, even as he swaps his trademark "How ya doin?'" with the staff at St. Joe's. Asked if there was poor organization when he came to the hospital, he replies: "It was more like non-organization. A lot of times you had to ask people to step up. You've got to show them that there's some redeeming value—that they're not going to be taken advantage of, that you appreciate what they're doing." As Mitchell is speaking, he is also reading the postoperative reports on two of his own patients and initialing them. It's the type of multi-tasking you might expect of him.

THERE IS SOMETHING bothering Eric Ignatius Mitchell, MD, MA, CPE. Mitchell is leading a visitor down a 4th-floor corridor in St. Joseph's Hospital, in the heart of one of Philadelphia's grittiest neighborhoods, talking about his efforts to get more dialysis machines, when he spots a tiny wad of paper on the linoleum floor. The former college basketball whiz, a lanky 6'6" tall, stoops over and lays it into to a nearby trash can. He turns to a hospital physician who is passing by and jokes, "I get an extra $1,000 every time I do that." Picking up litter is just one of the seemingly endless chores that Mitchell faces every day as Senior Vice President of Medical Affairs for North Philadelphia Health System. His ultimate mission is to turn around St. Joseph's, a once-struggling inner-city hospital, and two other health care facilities.

Just minutes before scooping up the trash, Mitchell stopped to reassure a patient's relative by speaking fluent Spanish, a language the 53-year-old orthopedist learned just a decade ago.

Now, Mitchell leads the visitor past a plaster-cast, thorn-bearing Jesus — one of the many icons that speak to the hospital's Roman Catholic legacy—to a window overlooking the bleak landscape of North Philadelphia's Girard Avenue and its shuttered row homes.....

"Philly Physician Executive Combats Big City Blight". Mitchell helps troubled hospital turn around, leads troops in his spare time. Will Bunch. The Philadelphia Daily News.

....Despite no money for college and little encouragement from his teachers, Eric Mitchell was determined to make something of himself. Ever since he got that plastic doctor kit when he was 7, he dreamed of becoming a physician.

Learn how he achieved that goal—and so much more.... is and decaying neighborhoods.

The Physician Executive Magazine. 20 November-December 2001.

....Expect from a person who essentially performs three full-time jobs. The sports-medicine expert still treats patients roughly 40 hours a week. Since he also became a top administrator at North Philadelphia Health System, St. Joseph's and its sister facility, Girard Medical Center, the facilities survived a wave of hospital closures in the Philadelphia region and are emerging from a fiscal morass that included bankruptcy back in the late 1980s. The system started turning profits around the time Mitchell arrived in 1994. The profits convinced the federal government to engineer a $24 million bailout package in 1997 that lowered the system's debt. Today, Mitchell proudly shows all his visitors a model of the hospital's dream for the future. It is a $24-million, six-story hospital building that North Philadelphia Health System wants to build on a parking lot across the street from its dingy current quarters that were built in the late 1970s. The new structure is a vision that's on hold right now.

Hoops and hopes. But if it's like any of Mitchell's other dreams, it won't stay unfulfilled for long. Mitchell decided he wanted to become a physician when he was just 7 years old, when his parents gave him a plastic doctor's kit as a present. The idea seemed like a long shot.

Mitchell was one of seven children growing up in a small apartment in a working-class section of Washington, D.C. His father, who worked on the D.C.-to-New York mail train, pushed his offspring to study hard but also made it clear there wouldn't be money to pay for college.

But Mitchell got several breaks early on. A member of the city's small community of black Roman Catholics, Mitchell was able to attend parochial schools in an era when the local public schools were still mostly still segregated and African-Americans were bussed to inferior classrooms.

Shortly before Mitchell entered high school, his dad took him to watch a high school basketball Phenom named Lew Alcindor and his Power Memorial team defeat a Washington-area Catholic school, DeMatha High. His father was gently dismissive when the boy, who was starting an adolescent growth spurt but had little hoops experience, said he wanted to attend DeMatha and play for its legendary coach, Morgan Wootten. But some months later, when the still-growing Mitchell entered DeMatha for his first day of classes, Coach Wooten tapped the surprised freshman from behind and told him to show up for practice.

So it was that Mitchell was on the court when DeMatha handed Power Memorial and the future Kareem Abdul-Jabbar the only loss of his storied high school career.

Actually, getting into medicine proved to be more of a struggle for Mitchell than playing basketball. It was the mid-1960s, and black students were typically steered away from Pre-Med courses. At DeMatha, a guidance counselor, John Moreland, even tried to convince him not to apply to college. "And I was on an advanced track, I had taken calculus, I had taken geometry, I had taken algebra, and two years of a language," Mitchell recalls. "And I thanked him but I told John Moreland that I was going to go on to college and be a physician. When I go back to DeMatha, I never let John call me "Iggy" or "Mitch" or "Eric"—I required him to call me "Dr. Mitchell". "And hopefully it was a lifetime lesson," Mitchell adds. "Don't ever underestimate the human mind and the human will."

Indeed, when Mitchell graduated from DeMatha in 1967, in the top 10 percent of his class, offers of full scholarships began pouring in from UCLA—where Alcindor went—North Carolina, Michigan and some southern colleges looking for an academic standout to integrate their all-white basketball teams.

Instead, Mitchell enrolled at St. Joseph's University (no affiliation with the hospital) in Philadelphia, a small Jesuit college that was known for producing doctors as well as a winning basketball team. The only black student living in the campus dorms for a time, Mitchell nevertheless thrived at St. Joe's and was ultimately accepted into the University of Pennsylvania's top-rated medical school.

Mitchell interned at Philadelphia General Hospital, a city-funded facility that's now closed. It catered primarily to a lower income clientele on the city's western side. "People said to me, 'Why are you going there?' and I said I believed it afforded me the opportunity of a lifetime. And it did." Nevertheless, his career path to serving Philadelphia's poor took a detour into orthopedics, which he studied as a resident at Penn. He worked on a research program that focused on making bone matter out of electricity and established a successful practice that involved everything from treating Olympians to patients with tennis elbow. He also made a home in the heart of Philadelphia's Center City, where he lives today with two sons, ages, 16 and 14.

"Don't ever underestimate the human mind and the human will."

The Physician Executive. November-December 2001.

....Guard duty. It was around this time that a colleague at Penn encouraged him (Dr. Mitchell) to join the National Guard. It marked the beginning of a 20-year military career for Mitchell, who is currently a colonel in the medical corps of the Army Reserve and also works with the Inspector General's office of the Department of Defense on health care issues. The job requires Mitchell to be willing to go anywhere on a moment's notice. That was the case in the fall of 1994.

One morning, a call came into his Philadelphia orthopedics office asking to speak with "Colonel Mitchell." "I said, 'Good morning, Colonel Mitchell here,'" and he said, 'Colonel, You are to report to

Fort Drum, New York, at 2200 hours. Any questions, please talk to a general.'

It turned out that Mitchell was on his way to Haiti, where U.S. troops helped restore democracy. He packed about 10 days' worth of clothes, but ended up staying as a medical advisor to top brass for about six months. Lucky break.

An accident of fate brought Mitchell to St. Joseph's and North Philadelphia Health System.

The struggling hospital had lost its only orthopedic surgeon. A patient from the neighborhood had fallen off a ladder and broken both his wrists, but he refused to let doctors in the emergency room transfer him to another hospital. St. Joseph's director of nursing tracked down Mitchell and begged him to come treat the patient, even though Mitchell didn't have privileges at St. Joe's. "I said I'm not even dressed. I'm in Bermuda pants and a khaki shirt. She said, 'Dr. Mitchell, we'll make all of the exceptions if you can help us.' I said, I'll be there in ten minutes." After that, officials at the health system started lobbying Mitchell to join the staff. It was then that the longtime orthopedic surgeon first considered making the move into administration. "Lord Baltimore once said that power only yields to one other thing—an equal or greater power," he recalls. "I said I would not come unless I could find a position in the institution where I could make a difference. I said orthopedics is easy enough to buy, but what I want to do is get into an organizational structure where I can make a difference." He learned that North Philadelphia Health System had gone without a vice president for medical affairs for two-and-one-half years.

Mitchell has rarely moved since he accepted the post. He quickly made recruiting young doctors to the hospital a top priority and he dramatically improved St. Joseph's rating from the state while sharply raising the percentage of minorities on the staff. He spurred the hospital to follow competitors and move toward performing most surgery on an outpatient basis, freeing up space in the cramped facility. He also learned to be something of a salesman—not much of a problem for someone with Mitchell's sense of self-confidence. He persuaded local businesses like Girard College—which is just several blocks away, but was sending ill students to a hospital many miles away on the city's western fringe—to begin working with St. Joseph's.

On his walking tour, he proudly shows off a patient room redone with pink curtains, a four-poster bed and a contemporary-art print. It's the result of a $5,000 gift from one of his patients.

The hospital's best ambassador.

More importantly, Mitchell is constantly thinking of ways to improve healthcare for people who live in one of the poorest zip codes in urban America. His latest project is a push for telemedicine where patients could use videoconferencing equipment at remote locations like community centers to speak with a physician, rather than come into the emergency rooms.

Even with his military mindset, he is beloved by the hospital staff. Workers from the cafeteria and other corners of the hospital stopped to hug Mitchell—who was celebrating his birthday that day—as he passed through. Catherine Kutzler, the CEO of St. Joseph's Hospital and a trained nurse, laughs as she talks about Mitchell's attempts

The Flow of Life

to bring Army style discipline to what was once a very chaotic health care facility. "It's that military personality— we've tried to break it," she chuckles. "And the cleanliness," Kutzler says Mitchell's greatest achievement is recruiting more African-Americans and other members of minority groups to work at St. Joseph's, which serves a predominantly black neighborhood. It's important "that the patients feel they are receiving care by someone who understands their culture."

In recent years, Mitchell plunged into learning more about "What I want to do is get into an organizational structure where I can make a difference."....

The Physician Executive. 22 November-December 200

Hospital administration, taking courses on finance and management issues.

....Earlier this year, Mitchell became a Certified Physician Executive. Running a big-city hospital isn't Mitchell's last or greatest ambition, however. A decade ago, he also earned a master's degree in international relations from Rhode Island's Salve Regina College. It was there that he learned to speak Spanish. He hopes to become an ambassador someday.

ACPE CareerLink is an on line service that can connect you to organizations and recruiters seeking qualified physician executives. At no charge, physician executives can conduct job searches across the nation by location or by employer. And, you can respond immediately by generating a resume and cover letter on-line, which will be delivered to the employer. You may also choose to post your resume for potential employers and recruiters to review. Plus, by designating the geographical criteria to which you have an interest in, you will receive an email when new jobs are added, with a link taking you directly to their location on the site. CareerLink is free to all physician executives seeking career opportunities…..

Chapter Twenty-One

A new commander for the 343rd CSH was found in New York and I am on my way to Puerto Rico to become the first off-Island commander of the 369th CSH in Puerto Nieva, PR. I had gotten my S1 and S3 their order for a transfer. They were there ahead of me. The 369th CSH had a long history in the United States Army but had never had a commander that was not from PR.

Shortly after my arrival and taking command of the 369th, I knew that I wanted to carry the same battle cry of "Combat Ready" with me. I wanted it now put it into Spanish and it became "Listo Para Combate". The credo was warmly received as I was. However, at first some parties would start speaking Spanish with me, the commander, as part of the subject matter. It only took once for me to enter into their discussion and reminding the parties that this was my island and my wife's family were both born here and I had been coming to every part of this island from east to south to the west for the last twenty years so, "speak with care".

My three years of command for this CSH saw many MEDREDS to many different countries. The 369th CSH shredded the Bad Boy title and because the "GO TO" unit for the United States Army Reserve Command (ARCOM). We had tours to Fort Gordon, and the National Training Center and were denoted to be the Best of the Best. This is where I have to give the credit for planning to my S-staff, Major Smithson, who was at the epicenter of this mass movement toward excellence. After I left for my next move in my military career, sorry to say, I couldn't take Major Gray Smithson with me. The Major on my departure from the Island was quick to be promoted to LTC and it was well deserved. Thank you LTC Gray Smithson for your loyal serve, Combat Ready!

My next Army move was to the Pentagon. I found an IMA slot at the Secretary of Defense, as a Deputy Inspector General (DIG). The title sounded a lot better than the job itself. It was all about audits and planning. Not much action for my blood. I was stationed in the Army and Navy Building across the street from the Pentagon. I had my weekend duty that weekend before the 9/11/2001 struck on the Pentagon, New York and the crash in Pennsylvania. Well action sprang to the horizon, with war plans in the making and I knew that because of my MOS as an orthopaedic surgeon I would soon have to be Combat Ready.

Remember, I am an orthopaedic surgeon and my status as a DIG with the Department of Defense was not going to trump my orthopaedic surgeon status in a time of war. The setting was outside of any unit structure, I had no command or control of my when, what, or where I would go if and when the call came. So it was time to take some command and control with some decision making. Back in Philadelphia, I was moving full force into what was then called telehealth. I was also looking to move from Medical Affairs at the Hospital to maybe becoming a Chief Operation Officer for a Hospital Corporation. I was doing interviews for this position advance when the Towers fell on 9/11. I also knew that this would more than likely kill my private practice in orthopaedics with a possible four to six month absence and rising malpractice costs in the City of Brotherly Love. So, I talked it over with my staff and I planned to close my private practice. I knew that taking a new job with war looming at any point would not be a good entry for any new job position. Being called to duty for four to six months was not going to be the best answer in my pursuit of my career advancement. Daddy always said, "When possible act and do not react because of someone acting on you."

I took action and first volunteered to go to Saudi Arabia for my four to six month tour of active duty. This tour would not start until late October of 2002. This is July, so I need to have a stream of income until I joined the Army's payroll on active duty. So, I looked into being a locum tenens. What is a locum tenens? Locum tenens is a Latin phrase that means "one holding a place." The term refers to a physician who temporarily practices in place of an absent provider when circumstances such as family, illness or other causes create the vacancy. Next, I connected with a locum tenens company. I was quickly called about a six- week request in Farmington, Maine, at Franklin Memory Hospital (FMH) for an orthopaedic surgeon and the question was, did I want to accept this assignment. I ask the recruiters to give me a day or two to look at my schedule. It was not really about my schedule but it was about what my dad had taught me.

I connected with a locum tenens company. There was a great six-week request in Farmington, Maine and did I want to accept it. I ask the recruiters to give me a day or two to look at my schedule.

My father always said, "Always know where you're going and you will avoid trouble when you get there." I had no idea where I was going or where Farmington, Maine was and I needed to do some reconnaissance. I got a weekend special fare and flew to Portland, Maine. I rented a car and drove about eight miles to this community hospital. It was not going to be about the hospital that I was interested in, but it was going to be about the people who made up this community hospital.

The people were beautiful. The people were friendly. I never went into the hospital. I just visited shops, restaurants and other places of business. By the time I boarded my return flight to Philly I knew I would say yes on Monday morning to the locum tenens company and I would take the six-week position at FMH.

I packed up and was in Maine for the next six weeks. The hospital was ready for me and the hospital had been short of an orthopaedic surgeon for some time and there was some backlog. I was able to jump into this backlog and win over the OR staff on my abilities to get this done. About five weeks into my locum tenens stay, I got word that things in Iraq, the possible next AO for military action, were changing minute by minute. The then Secretary of State, General Colin Powell, got the President of the United States of America to go to the United Nations for resolution on these global boiling issues of possible weapons of mass destruction.

These proceedings at the UN push back the time-line for any military action. FMH asked if I would extend my six-week stay in this locum tenens position. I extended four times over the next seven months before I got the call to Active Duty. On March 12, 2003, at 1900 hr., I got a phone call that I was to report to Fort Sam Houston in Texas in forty-eight hours, in support of the 348th General Hospital.

I explained that I was not at my normal duty station of Philadelphia but I was working in Farmington, Maine. I was not in any unit so it was going to be hard to jockey for more time. I asked one of the

The Flow of Life

nurses in the Intensive Care Unit, who had friended me, if she had a garage. The answer was, yes, I have a garage. I then explained that the flag had to be raised, the call to duty had gone up and I needed to break down my apartment of seven months duration and be on a flight to Philadelphia in the morning. Do you know how much stuff you can collect in seven months? Of course, I owed Nurse CB a special thank you for the storage of my stuff in a hurry and assured her she was helping to serve God and Country.

After touching down in Philadelphia, Pennsylvania, the next morning, I would have just a couple of hours to see and kiss the kids and my wife and head back to the airport and head for Texas and Fort Sam Houston. I got my weapon, my protective gear and wheels were up again. I got to Texas and reported for duty. There was now a big push to get the 348th General Hospital up to full functional capacity. Within thirty-six hours of touching ground, wheels were up again and this time on to Ramstein Air Force Base in Germany.

I would spend the next ninety days in support of the War on Terror from the largest military hospital outside the United States of America. I had a telehealth assignment where I would evaluate wounded soldiers and determine if they needed to be shipped back to the receiving hospital in Germany. This was done by day and the planes would arrive by night.

….If you can keep your head when all about you

Are losing theirs and blaming it on you….

IF – by Rudyard Kipling

I made one trip home during that time to see my oldest son, Justin, graduate from high school. I promised him that I would be there, and I was. As previously mentioned, Justin had been selected to attend this magnet school and he had done very well. He was proud when his dad showed up in uniform, but the truth was I was more proud of him in his cap and grown. Justin had shined in academics and in sports and, as a father, I could not ask for more.

The fall of Baghdad, Iraq, was the start of a new campaign for me where I needed to get out of Germany and get back home to pull together what was left of my practice and determine my next step. I knew that I was not going to return to Philly for I had closed my practice there but sought a new locum tenens job somewhere in Pennsylvania to get restarted because I still had my youngest son in high school. I knew all too well how important those years between fifteen years of age and manhood where. The oldest was off to start college at DePaul University in Chicago, Illinois, in September, so I had one college bound and one to go.

I came home from Germany and got a job in Sayer, Pennsylvania, at Robert Packer Hospital. This was a locum tenens job that would become a permanent position for the next four years. I was able to get my youngest son to come to Sayer, Pennsylvania, and switch to a local high school. Marcus loved the game of basketball as much as I did and he started playing the game with an eye on following his dad. Well, we had three great years together before college. I taught him the principles instilled in me by Coach Wootten and how to target jump as Frank F had taught me many years earlier. I taught him how to play defense. I taught him how to take an offensive charge to take a scoring opportunity away from the opponent. He learned all the rest and could shoot and score way better than his father.

The Flow of Life

My telehealth world had again followed me home from active duty in Europe like it did from my 1994 Haiti deployment. The civilian side of my telehealth expansion was expanded when I got a call form Kurt. Kurt said that he had just bought out the rights to Doctors Telehealth Network (DTN). I had invested a pretty dollar into that company and now it was gone. But maybe not! Kurt continued to say that the only thing that he wanted from DTN, which he had re-named Physicians Telehealth Network (PTN), was me! He asked if I would help him promote this concept because he was going after an eleven million dollar grant/loan from the United States Department of Agriculture (USDA).

I explained where I was and what I was doing. He thought Pennsylvania was the perfect venue for this program. I was now at a rural hospital in Northeastern Pennsylvania with a lot of nursing homes and rural clinics that were many miles apart. I got several projects started and even did a postsurgical telehealth clinic, which was over fifty miles one way for surgical follow-ups which cut the distance and gas usage for many postoperative patients. Kurt just about lived with my son and me during the next two years. We were able to start a number of telehealth programs with other regional healthcare centers under my medical directorship. I was able to work with the former Secretary of Aging for the Commonwealth of Pennsylvania. We wrote a paper together during that time that was published in Physician Executive magazine. We were still denoted as early adapters in the telehealth world.

....If you can wait and not be tired of waiting....

IF – by Rudyard Kipling

In Marcus's junior year of basketball, he got better with every game. He worked hard and made the all-star team at the end of the year. That summer he ate, slept and played basketball. For his senior year he took his team to become undefeated and Marcus was the MVP for his region. Marcus and I were living in a region of Pennsylvania that did not get a look from major universities in the basketball world. Oh, yes, he had a number of regional coaches looking at him and those schools were Division II and Division III schools.

The end of the season came and the time to decide where he wanted to go to college was upon us. I told my son, as my father had told me, it was time for him to make some decisions about where he wanted to go to college and where he wanted to play his basketball. Marcus started this discussion off by saying that he did not want to play Division III basketball. I understood that and said, "Well, you have a number of Division II schools that want you." "Yes," he said, "but I don't want to play Division II basketball." Ok, I said, "but you didn't get any Division I offers, principally because of the region that you played in."

Marcus, looked at me and said, "You played Division I and I want to play Division I". "Ok," I said, "where". Then he said, "Where you played". Then my legs went weak, and tears formed in the corners of my eyes. "Well", I said. "Your mother and I have put away money for your education and for you to go to any school you desire. And if that is where you want to go, let's make it happen. However, you making the team and playing for a Division I basketball team is on you and your desire."

My two sons, Justin and Marcus, had heard my Double D lecture enough times that they could give it. Dedication and Determination were the two elements that you needed in order to rise to the top. I had taught them if they could be "All IN" with these two principles then the world was their oyster.

….Yours is the Earth and everything that's in it,

And –which is more–you'll be a Man my son....

IF – by Rudyard Kipling

Well, "Mr. Marcus" applied both of these principles and made the team as a walk-on for St. Joseph's University, Division I basketball team, thirty-nine years after I made that same team. This was a very sweet moment and point of time in my life. Marcus played well and went on to become the go-to person to set the offenses and defenses of the opposing team for the next two years. However, after two years, Marcus went to the basketball coach and asked for a scholarship for his efforts. The coach explained that he had no available scholarships. Marcus made a man size decision to not to play his next two years. For him, it was a value proposition. He did not believe that he was getting the value out of the effort that he was putting in. Marcus followed the team closely because a bunch of these guys were his friends.

Now, both boys are in college and it's about time for another move. I had put my VideoHealthDx™, at that time noted as Telehealth, on the back burner for some time. Trauma orthopaedics carries a high risk factor and I am now approaching sixty years of age. I started to look for new jobs that will allow me to develop my VideoHealthDx™ concepts and interest. I found a new job offer in Maine where I vowed to return someday after I left for my tour of duty in the War on Terror in 2003. The job would allow me to develop the concept of VideoHealth™ in the worker compensation arena. I took that job about one year after my youngest was off to college. I was heading back to Maine.

Chapter Twenty-Two

I started my new job as Medical Director of Concentra Medical Center, Bangor, Maine, just before the 4th of July of that year. I was living in a furnished apartment with plans to build an off-the-grid home, ASAP. With major surgery out of my plate for the first time in thirty-five years, I put all of that energy into the building of my new house. I planned and built every part of the house that I could do and contracted out all the rest. The house got started in November and I moved in from my on-site trailer in March because the house had heat. However, the house was by no means finished. Over the next several months, working full time as the Medical Director for a work health and urgent care Center, I finished the inside of the house and was able to move in my furniture which had been in storage for almost one year.

As the new medical director, I defined to my boss, what I wanted in the deal for coming to Maine. I would take this medical center, which was ranked about 187/340 clinics to the top ten percent in my first eighteen months. In return, my boss had to pave the way for me to set up and develop a regional Telehealth program for the parent company. The deal was struck. I used all of my leadership training and proceeded to reach and surpass my goal in the first fourteen months of my arrival. At month fourteen, the rankings for these 340 clinics were published and our Bangor Medical Center was ranked number one of 340 clinics in the country.

Now, I was to get my regional telehealth center. The plans and money was allocated for its tip off. Two months before the launch, my boss dropped dead on his bedroom floor. This doctor was one of the regional vice presidents that had oversight for about twenty percent of the entire clinics in the United States. Things went into a downward spiral and in six months my telehealth program was on hold. I was on the way out the door with all $60,000 of my own personal telehealth equipment that I had lent the organization to start the telehealth program.

....If you can dream –and not make dreams your master....

IF – by Rudyard Kipling

My VideoHealthDx™ dreams are out in front of me. I am sixty-two years old. I have just retired from the United States Army after twenty-three years. I have my 401, which got reduced to a 201, with 2007-8 hits. I do not want another job of working for anyone else. Fate intervenes. I get a phone call from a doctor friend of forty years, Dr. H. She wanted me to look at a Videophone that she thinks would be good for my Telehealth. I inquire about the cost and functionality. Only the price was known. Remember, I just pulled my equipment out of the medical center and it was only good for point-to-point connection. My doctor friend tells me that this device is $100. I am thinking that this device is a toy because my equipment just six to nine years earlier cost me $15,000 to $18,000 dollars each. I had two video conferencing devices and the major part of my $60,000 of equipment that I had just recovered from my old job.

With doubt brimming for the $100 device, I agreed to take a look at it. A plan was made to ship me one of these videophones for me to try. An Independent Business Owner, LD, from New Hampshire shipped the shipped the Videophone the next day. After two phone calls and some basic research on the parent company, I was "ALL IN". Mind you, this phone came from a direct sales company, but the parent company also had a telephone company that was analog and digital phone service around the world. I had been studying the advances in the Voiceover Internet Protocol (VoIP). Now, I had in my hands Video and Voice over Internet Protocol (V-VoIP).

However, I knew nothing, and I mean nothing, about direct sales. But I did not care because I could see a videophone in every home with the doctor on the other end. The journey had begun.

I spent my day going to community events to find people that might have some interest in my concept of VideoHealth with weekly meetings. I was in an organization that I knew nothing about. I had to find some training for this venture. That same nurse who rescued my stuff the day I deployed for the War on Terrorism, six years earlier, was still in the picture now as my significant other after a divorce took the boys' mother out of the marriage picture. Carmen is her name and again she came to my rescue again. This time it was her social media connection where she found someone that was also doing the same company and was having meetings in Portland, Maine. I had been traveling 4 hours to New Hampshire for training because I knew no one in Maine doing this direct marketing business.

Using a format that I used when I learned the game of basketball, you find the best players and play with them. I was going to do the same in this new game. First, I needed to get trained and develop the needed skill sets, just like in surgery. Then I had to find the best mentor in this business. I had an international training event for this company that was coming up and I knew that I need to attend if I was going to understand this new business model that I knew very little about. I told Carmen that I was going to go to San Diego. She expressed no interest in the business but did have an interest in going to the San Diego Zoo which she had always wanted to visit. So, together we headed to San Diego with separate agendas, direct sales vs. the Zoo. Attending the convention by day with me and 20,000 other attendees, it only took until the end of the second day of the convention for a new mindset to take hold, the start of a shocking new adventure.

Walking back to our hotel after the second day, Carmen said. "Eric, I want to join you." I said, "You are with me, what do you mean?" She said I like this company and I want to join with you in this company and learn something new and exciting. Carmen joined Team Vision to ACtioN that day and at the time of this writing she is at the fifth highest position in this company. I have no doubt that she will reach the top of this company with me. And, she is now my wife. We are true partners in life and business. My family is now complete with the addition of the two daughters that I never had—Isabella and Brianna.

Chapter Twenty-Three

I have taken the credo concept from my army days and made "ALL IN" the battle cry for this residual income model of capital. All this talk of residual income and capital are a result of more than 300 audiobooks done over the last four years. This has been my on-the-job training in addition to going to every quarterly convention in the last four years. It took me about a year and a half before I was able to see the donut and not the hole in this business. This saying comes from my dad again. He always said, "Son as you rumble through life and whatever your goal, keep sight of the donut and not of the hole." Those two words, whole and hole, can be life up close or from afar. This was one of those life lessons that keep coming back to you.

I will admit that when I got into the direct sales business I didn't have the 20,000 foot view and was so in love with video device because of long term quest to put a doctor into every home, I could only see the hole of VideoHealth™ and not the whole picture of lavage and distribution for essential services and energy. I have since learned about social media, social networking, personal relationships and the power of one.

I have since also built a team of over two hundred other independent business owners and I am now a "Change Agent" for people who want to change their lives. I want to change the way people live their lives. Allowing them to dream again and break the glass ceiling, I want to teach people how to stop trading time for money in a job and start building a plan B of residual income and financial independence.

Leverage is the key word here. Mind you, I was born in the middle of the 20th Century, and I was told to go to school, get a good education and go and get a good job. I did all of the above. I was a first generation college graduate. I was a first generation into professional schools. So, from my generational viewpoint I did everything I was supposed to do and then some.

My children were born at the end to the 20th century and so many things have changed. The socially crafted government program like Social Security and Medicare have run into sustainability problems because of the large aging population and our present increased life expectancy. This book is for that generation and the next generation that comes after them.

….If you can think –and not make thoughts your aim….

IF – by Rudyard Kipling

To write down your objectives increases your chances of success eight fold. I wanted to give our team something to build on. Incomes equals outcome.

I wrote a short blog every day for over two years to keep myself and others engaged. I have more than 700 blogs to share. Maybe this will be my second book.

Because my dad was such a driving force in my development, I reference him all the time. Included in this book are a short number of blogs where my dad's sayings and philosophy were used as a teaching point.

The End

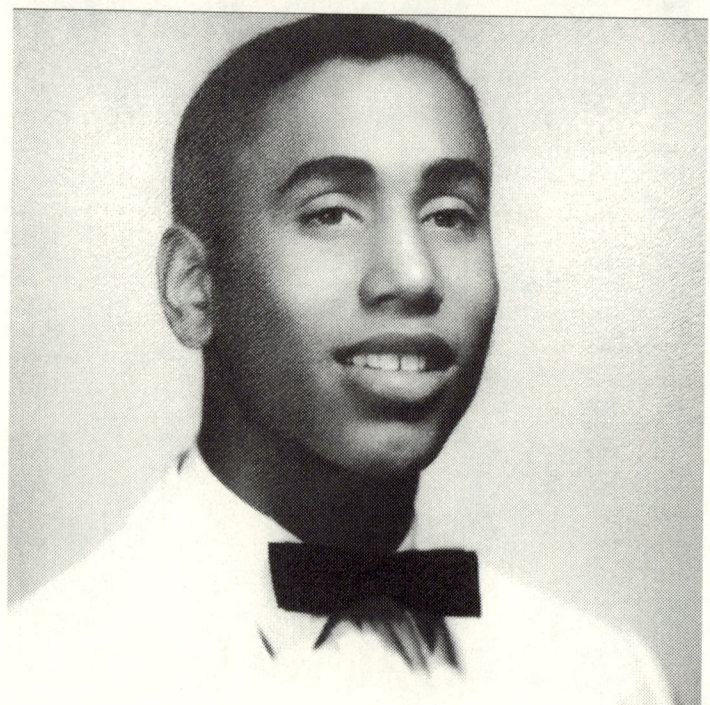

VNIVERSITAS
PENNSYLVANIENSIS
OMNIBVS HAS LITTERAS LECTVRIS SALVTEM DICIT

Cum academiis antiquis mos sit scientiis literisve
humanioribus excultos titulo iusto condecorare
nos igitur auctoritate Curatorum nobis commissa

ERIC IGNATIVS MITCHELL

ob studia a Professoribus approbata ad gradum

MEDICINAE DOCTORIS

admisimus eique omnia iura honores privilegia ad hunc
gradum pertinentia libenter concessimus
Cuius rei testimonio nomina nostra die mensis
Maii xx Anno Salutis MCMLXXXIV et Vniversitatis
conditae ccxxxivPhiladelphiae subscripsimus

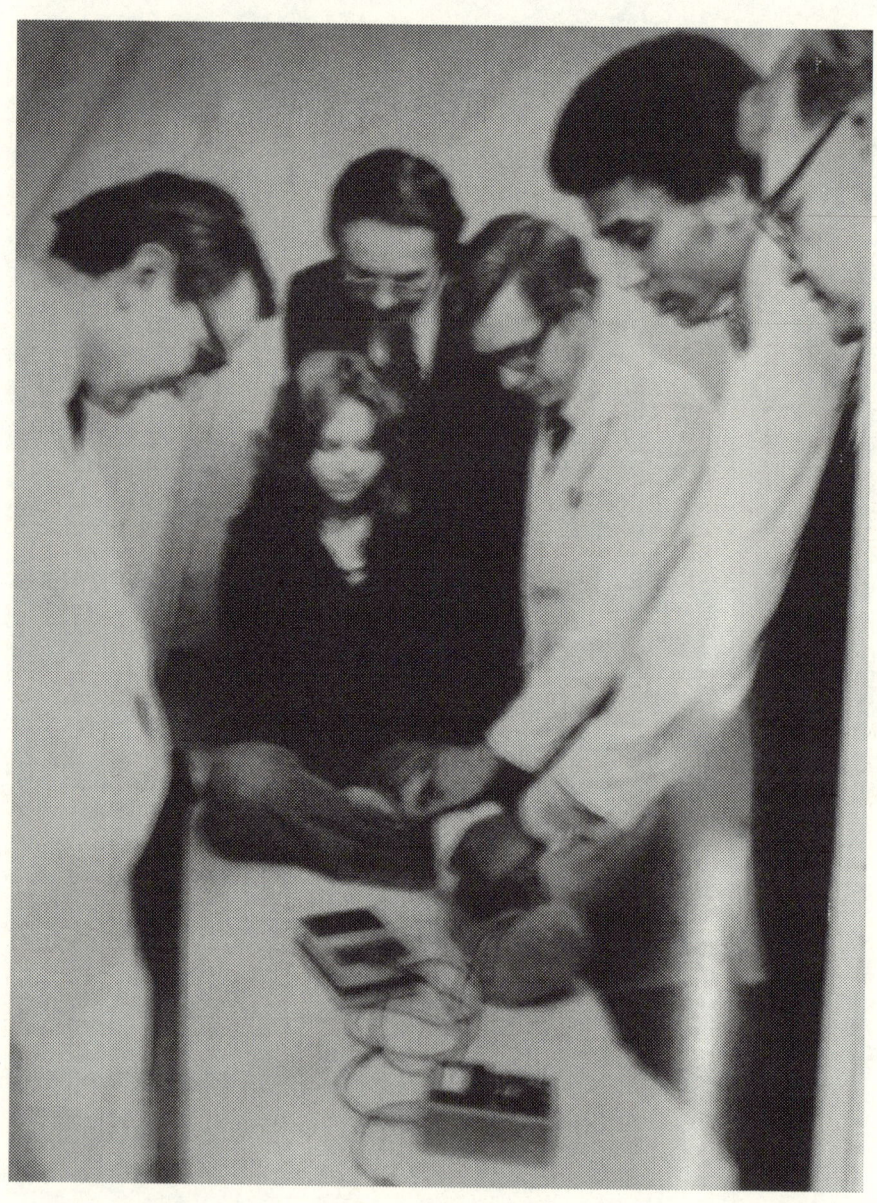

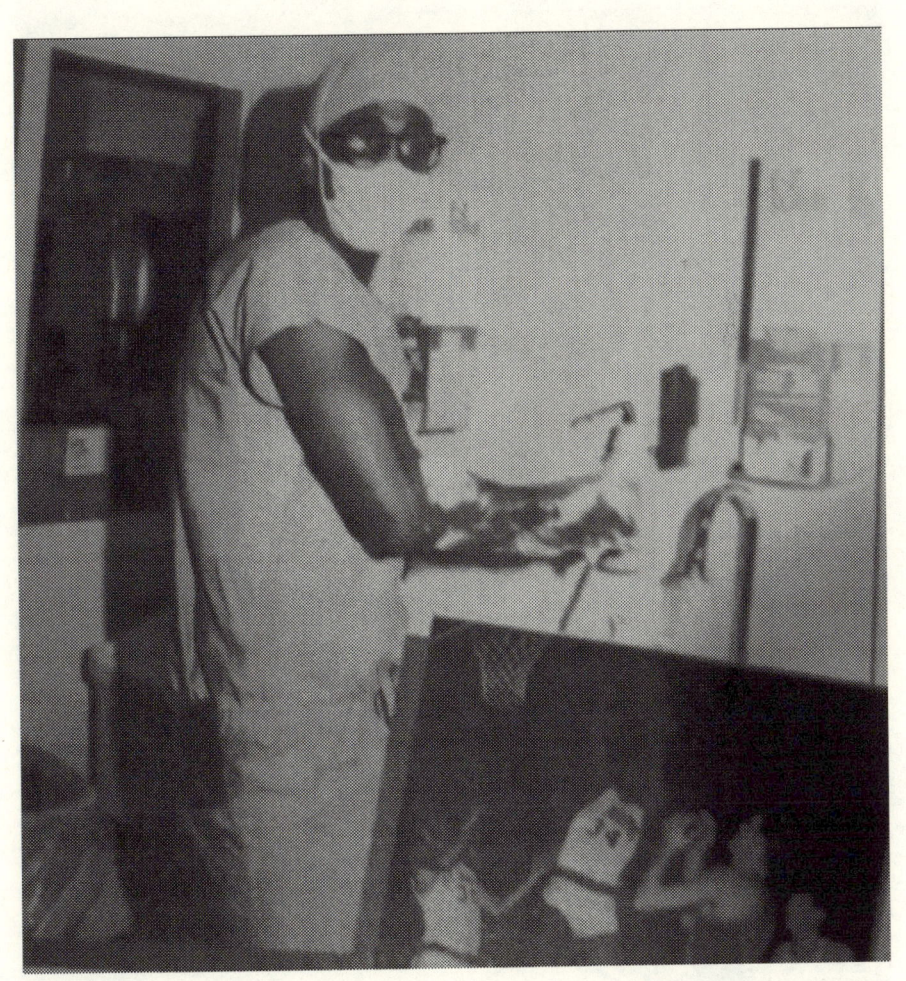

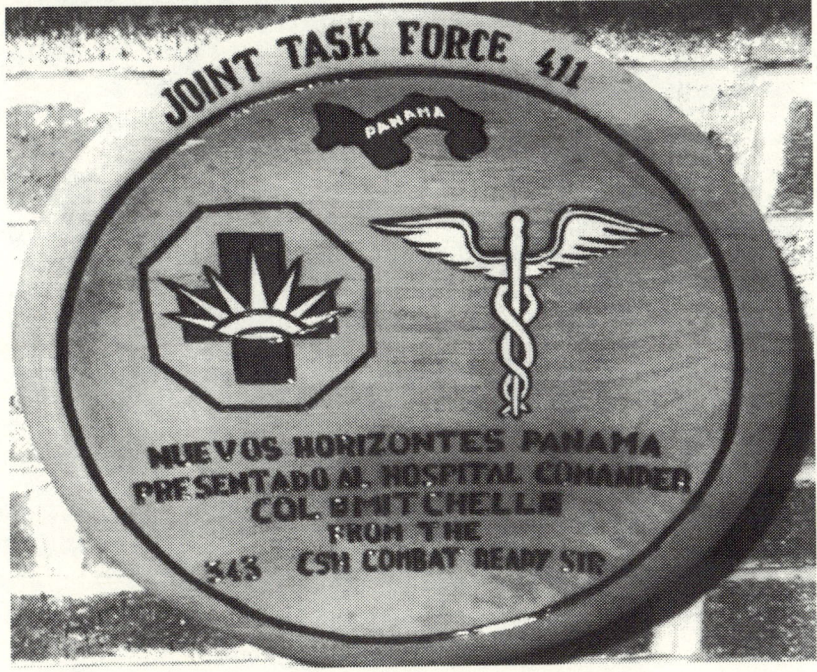

The DeMatha Alumni Association

The DeMatha Distinguished Alumnus Award

Dr. Eric I. Mitchell '67

Presented on September 25, 1999

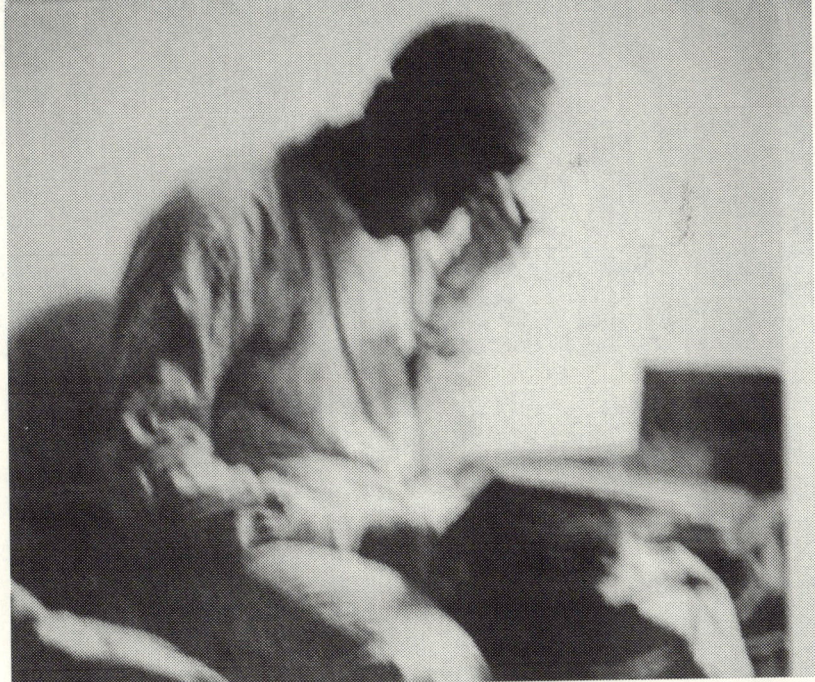

Printed in the United States
By Bookmasters